ALL MEN are DOGS

IT IS WHAT IT IS.

WRITTEN BY

KEVIN ELLIOTT

EDITED BY MARCHET DENISE FULLUM

K. E. PUBLISHING

ALL MEN ARE DOGS

It Is What it Is!

ISBN: 978-0-9960248-0-8

Edited By: Marchet Denise Fullum

Graphics and Illustrations By: Jessica Godbee

Published By: KE Publishing

For Bookings or Orders

Therealallmenaredogs@gmail.com

Instagram: All Men Are Dogs

Therealallmenaredogs@gmail.com

TheRealAllMenAreDogs.com

Contents

ALL MEN
are
D**O**GS
IT IS WHAT IT IS.

All Men *ARE* Dogs!

It has been said that a dog is man's Best Friend. So, it's only fitting that women put their stamp on this by claiming, "**All Men *Are* Dogs.**" I sat and pondered that thought for a minute and it hit me that they, women, may be on to something. We *are* dogs in the truest sense of the word! Look at any dog, observe how it interacts, communicates, eats, and sleeps. Pay close attention to all of its good qualities and bad habits. You might be surprised by how many similarities to your man there are. It's undeniable.

Women love to fool themselves and think they will settle for nothing less than the "perfect" man. However, society and technology have transformed the world we call home and many women find themselves chasing after the myth of perfection instead of accepting the fact that <u>no one is perfect</u>.

Believing you can find "perfection" creates unrealistic expectations that can only lead to unhappiness. Women have to learn that with love, just like everything else in life, they have to take the good with the bad.

Once women know that all men are not perfect creatures, they can stop looking for their "prince" to come and take them away in a horse-drawn carriage. It's **not** happening, ladies!

The Toltec philosophy says, "Humans live in a permanent dream state. Making things exactly what they think they should be, judging everything they lay their eyes upon from the onset, and seeing things the way they want to see them."

It's vital for women to see that all dog breeds have individual styles and traits. In fact, they even have swagger that cannot be overlooked. Dogs have human characteristics that are consistent with men and women. These characteristics can cause mixed emotions —ones that can make you laugh, cry, show signs of intelligence, and ones that can manipulate a situation to the dog's advantage.

Whether you are married, single, divorced, or most importantly if you're the "Bitter Woman," your prayers have been answered! This book will be the guide that helps you see the undeniable parallel between dogs and men. As you read this book you will be able to identify yourself, your partner, and your possible situation, and then learn what it takes to understand what's going on.

As women, it is important that you *keep it real* with yourself and see things in *black and white* — sometimes, there is no room for shades of gray. So, let us start with that little misused phrase, "keeping it real." The key to that phrase starts with you. Yes, I said *you*!

Sorry ladies, but I have to lay down a few rules before we get started, because most women don't keep it real with each other — no matter the duration of the friendship. This is why some women like to have male friends who tell it to them straight without the sugar coating.

THE RULES OF ENGAGEMENT FOR *ALL MEN ARE DOGS*:

RULE #1

Please be objective and truthful with yourself.

Being objective allows you to go through this book without criticizing each line or looking for an excuse to explain why the situation described is not your situation. (I call doing this the "Not Me Syndrome" and that condition can be contagious — Airborne!)

RULE #2

Please, <u>NO</u> Hasty Decisions.
(Don't get mad at him! *You* picked him!)

Do not make any hasty, emotional decisions if you realize you are possibly living a lie or worse yet, wasting your precious time. Like I said, don't get mad at him — you picked, groomed, washed and fed him. I'm not saying you're stuck with him, just don't be upset with him for being exactly who he is. Like anything else in life, you've got to adjust and accept the fact that he really "*is what he is!*" Once you're aware of this and know that you cannot change anyone, you can make your relationship better. Life is about structure, foundation, discipline, and decision-making. Remember, Rome was not built in a day so give yourself a break. Even if it doesn't initially look good for the home team, don't panic.

RULE #3

Self Inventory (point no fingers)

Self-inventory is always in order. Subtle changes in *you* produce major changes in *your* life. Your attitude and disposition have a lot to do with how you make decisions. It's simple: your bad attitude and/or negative disposition contribute to what you may be laying next to every night. *Hello!*

These rules of engagement had to be set because this book might sting a little. I wanted to give you the chance to brace and prepare yourself for the realizations that will take place while you're reading **All Men Are Dogs**.

El Problemo

When looking for a man, most women have unreasonable and unrealistic expectations. When you ask a woman the famous question, "What do you want in a man?" her answer will continuously change as she moves through each phase of her life. Below, we have listed some typical answers women give to this question. I don't have the space or

THINGS WOMEN SAY THEY WANT IN A MAN...

Funny	Bald Head	Smart
Tall	A Provider	Needy
Skinny	A Thug	Muscular
Athletic	Short	Educated
Bossy	Has a Beard	Thoughtful
	Kinky in Bed	

energy to name every single possibility because every woman has her own list, but I included things I've heard mentioned often.

A woman's preferences might change drastically as she enters a new phase in her life, in other words as she grows and matures, the type of man she wants in her life will change. For example, in her 20s she might want a tall, good-looking man with short hair, and have no regard for his earning potential, but when she enters her 30s she might find she's suddenly attracted to a short, bald man who has a great job and a vacation house. GO FIGURE. What's more, the image of her "dream man" will probably change again when she reaches 40 and, if she still hasn't found her life mate, that image will continue to evolve as she ages and accumulates life experiences.

At the end of the day, what all women really want is a "good" man. The problem is that *every* woman wants this, making demand high and supply extremely low—almost to the point where women will sacrifice many of the things they thought they needed in a man as long as he's "aiight" and has a full set of teeth. Even the coveted muscles become optional when it comes to choosing between looks and a man's character.

If you've already found your man but your relationship isn't what you'd hoped, it could be because you don't feel complete as a woman. This incomplete feeling will affect your relationship and is probably causing most of the problems you're experiencing. I'm not saying the man doesn't have a part in the confusion and strife, but you have to admit that women are usually the key to a healthy relationship.

Another common problem occurs when a woman attempts to change the man she's with so he fits her image of perfection. What she is really trying to do is make her man into something he is not, and that is where everything starts to go wrong. She isn't willing to accept that he is who he is. Let me repeat that last part ... *he is who he is*. Don't be this woman!

You can bring out good qualities in your man or even upgrade him a bit, but you can't make him into something he isn't, no matter how hard you try. When life gives you lemons … yes, make lemonade — but be reasonable, ladies, only Jesus turned water into wine!!!

Dogs come in a variety of shapes, sizes, colors, and personalities, and men are no different. The similarities don't end there — they also like to be treated the same way. It tickles my fancy when I see women who have a pet they'll do anything for, including driving all the way across town for special treats, going for walks in the cold, etc. They constantly lavish attention on this pet and treat it better than most humans in their lives. WOW!!! Why would you treat your pet better than your man? What's up with that?

Just as I can tell the difference between a neglected dog and a healthy dog and a dog that's loved verses a dog that gets no affection, I can see the same things in a neglected man and one who's treated well. The treatment the dog receives is always written in his eyes — the same goes for a man. Think about it!

Ladies, you need to realize that men are simple creatures. They are basically satisfied with the necessities in life, i.e. food, water, a

7

few toys to play with, a space to roam, a lot of love, and a whole lot of affection. This is the recipe for keeping the peace. It's simple — no magic or miracles involved. If you're in a relationship, try providing just the necessities for a week and see how peaceful your life can be. You'll come to understand that some men, just like dogs, can be trained and led to a calm state of mind — all it takes is a little care and praise from you. However, just as some dogs can never be trained, there are some men who can never become "good" men. If this is your man, you can try to coexist with him and just hope he doesn't go off or you can move on and find a truly good man.

A word of warning, ladies: remember, another women can read this book and use it to fool, trap, and capture your "good" man. The funny thing about that is, being the good guy he is he won't even realize that he's nothing more than a trophy to her — women like this are in it for the chase not the long haul. You probably won't need to worry about this "other" woman as long as you follow my rules — you'll win the battle as long as you're providing all his necessities.

At the end of the day, if you understand your breed of dog (man), and know how to care for, love, nurture, and maintain him, then you'll have happiness and a "pet" for a life. This bears repeating: *If you understand your breed of _man_, and know how to care for, love, nurture, and maintain him, then you'll have happiness and a _man_ for life.*

In the following pages, I'll teach you about the different breeds of dogs, their personality traits, what you can expect from them and what you need to do to find the right "breed" for you.

THE GERMAN SHEPHERD

Kids can be a good thing with the German Shepherd man. He will do everything possible to keep it together. Even if you think he might step out of character one day, he definitely will not if kids are in the equation. The kids will see him as a model hard-worker and use him as their foundation.

The German Shepherd

The German Shepherd man is the prototypical male. I like to refer to him as the "man without a face." The German Shepherd man is the ultimate guy women dream about; the one who makes you and your girlfriends melt because he's such a great guy. The good news, ladies, is that there are still a few of these old-fashioned German Shepherds around.

The German Shepherd man is loyal and obedient. He thrives on challenging activities and is up for many tasks. He looks stern and imposing and makes an effective deterrent to opposing dogs and men alike. Just like an actual German shepherd he is a good provider, natural protector, and a potential non-cheater.

You will need to prepare yourself for a routine lifestyle with this man, but he will be completely trusting and loyal. He may even bring his entire check home to you and let you manage the household…imagine that.

Most women who have a relationship with a German Shepherd man are faced with this decision: Do I want adventure around every corner or can I deal with a predictable routine for the rest of my life?

Life with a German Shepherd man may not be exciting, but sometimes boring can be nice and safe. The German Shepherd man is the way he is because he is safe within the box of his life. That's not saying he doesn't see potential temptations; he just chooses to stay in his lane and ignore them.

Everyone has a weakness or vulnerable moment now and then, and in this life there are never any true guarantees, however the German Shepherd man is focused and there is very little anyone can do to come between him and his home life.

Not all German Shepherd men are born that way. Sometimes, he has already "been there and done that" and makes the transformation into a German Shepherd because of his past experiences. Other men have been German Shepherds their entire lives and are happy to stay that way. Regardless of how he got there, the German Shepherd man can sense danger and knows how to dodge it better than all other dog breeds.

SEX DRIVE

If you like routine, the German Shepherd man is the one for you. It's that same ole same ole with him — like a song on repeat. After a while, you'll know what's coming next.

I'm not saying that the same old thing is a bad thing. In fact, it can be a great thing, as long as you don't expect anything crazy in the bedroom.

Any change warrants a discussion with this man. My advice to you is to keep things the same. Do not venture out on this dog. If you do, the pure excitement of a spontaneous new situation plus a little adrenalin will make you absolutely "hate your freakin' life."

The key to a happy relationship with a German Shepherd man is *faithfulness*. So, ladies, turn in your player's card and throw in the white towel with this man. In a nutshell, "you can't miss what you never had."

THE ROTTWEILER

Kids with the Rottweiler man can be good. They might light a fire under him and motivate him to reach for his potential. Even if his goals are not fully obtained, he will have the ability to guide a child to a better life.

The Rottweiler

The Rottweiler man has characteristics similar to the German Shepherd man; however this man has a little extra spice. The Rottweiler is a natural born protector, loyal to a point, somewhat athletic and overall not a bad catch. The Rottweiler man is hard-working, a good provider, and is able to do multi-task.

Mirroring his canine counterpart, this man is territorial — protective of his home and family. You can feel secure and confident when spending time with him. The Rottweiler man is loyal to an extent — to what extent really depends on you. This is the type of man that can put a female's man-keeping skills to a test.

Even though he is not the only good dog to seek, the Rottweiler man offers a little more excitement mixed with his routine than most other catch-worthy men.

When involved in a relationship, the loyalty of the Rottweiler is solely with his female. Keep him occupied with enough toys and distractions and he won't get bored. If you're pursuing or involved with a Rottweiler man, you must have a few key components in the relationship to keep the love flowing.

The Rottweiler is a semi-intellectual, so you must be able to communicate with him on a variety of subjects to keep him mentally stimulated. If this isn't your thing, you may want to stay abreast of world events and the news.

The Rottweiler man is also semi-athletic, which means you must be into health, wellness, and sports. He may not be a true health fanatic but he is a believer in healthy living. He just might not be as consistent as he would like to be. Participating in a workout schedule out may be a plus on your resume when involved with the Rottweiler man.

Finally, he is a hard worker, maybe even a workaholic, so you must have some pep in your step and the spark of an industrious spirit because he deeply despises a lazy woman!

The Rottweiler man may seem like a lot of work, and maybe he is. Understanding and fulfilling his special needs will help you understand him and make for a better relationship. If this type of relationship maintenance is fine with you, then you will do fine with a Rottweiler, German Shepherd or similar personality type. If this isn't for you, read on to find your low maintenance breed.

The Rottweiler man is loyal when he feels that loyalty is returned, so be sure he knows you're there for him in every way. If you lack communication skills, then your Rottweiler man will surely lose interest and probably wander off to find a new adventure to quench his thirst.

Nevertheless, he never forgets his home. So, if you are involved with a Rottweiler man, don't mistake him for a German Shepherd who only wants his routine. You will have to step out of the routine box with spontaneity once in a while. This will keep your Rottweiler's mind on you, as his favorite toy, even when you aren't around.

SEX DRIVE

The Rottweiler man is semi-intellectual and athletic, so he will find ways to do new things in the bed. Whether his inspiration comes from a movie, an article, or via the Internet, he will get creative. He has an insatiable desire to be romantically involved and intimate, probably more than most men. So, it may take more than average affection to keep him satisfied.

THE DOBERMAN

Having kids can be the best thing since sliced bread for the Doberman man. This can be a major distraction for you but gives him peace of mind and a new focus. He will keep the child happy to keep you happy.

5

The Doberman

The Doberman man is like a chameleon, so you need to pay close attention to this section if you think this describes your man. He can adapt to any relationship style and any woman and he knows how to maneuver in every situation.

Mr. Debonair Doberman is crafty, conniving, and the king of manipulation. He's so good at it that you might not know everything he's been up to until the end of the relationship — or maybe never.

Have you ever been to a funeral where one woman is crying way too much? She seems devastated by the guy's death — like her heart's breaking, but no one at the funeral knows who she is. Everyone is suspicious, but no one knows for sure what her relationship with good old Uncle Edward was. This might be a clue that the dearly departed was a Devious Doberman man who had a little lady on the side!

The Doberman man is the type who has no conscience, meaning he doesn't feel guilty about what he's doing and can take the secrets of his indiscretions to his grave. He is sleek and on his game. Doberman's tend to gravitate toward jobs that keep odd hours or require travel, like police officer, doctor, lawyer, or truck driver, etc. because they help him camouflage his extracurricular activities. The combination of this man's appearance, occupation and serious demeanor will work together to help him hide his true nature.

A relationship with a Doberman man may start out perfect as far as you're concerned. Like any relationship, it has its ups and downs, but it seems normal and healthy. Over time, the Doberman has mastered how to handle you and keep you happy, which allows him room to maneuver without your knowledge within the relationship.

This maneuvering might not happen right away, it all depends on how fluid you are in your day-to-day schedule. Law #48 from the book *48 Laws of Power* says: "You should assume formlessness." When in a relationship with a Doberman man, this means you shouldn't be too predictable!

You may have to be rigid with your dog as well, meaning you stand for something and have morals and principles that cannot be changed, even by him. Your Doberman is so crafty, though, that he will constantly try get around your rules.

The Doberman man is usually a good judge of character and puts this to use when selecting his main woman. His choice is usually a sweet, non-antagonistic female. He wants someone who doesn't ask a lot of pressing questions or bother him about what he's been doing too much. The Doberman needs a woman like this because he doesn't want to be interrogated, even when he isn't doing anything he shouldn't.

He is also selective when choosing his *second* woman — his mistress. In this situation, his mistress usually knows about his main lady and plays up her willingness to do everything she can to keep her man comfortable and at ease about the game he's running. By being a willing participant, she hopes to gain favor and eventually advance to the number-one spot.

The crazy thing about the Doberman man is lack of guilt — he truly doesn't believe he's doing anything wrong. Wow! Isn't that amazing? Women do this too, but we'll talk about them in the next book. ☺

In a nutshell, the Doberman man lives his life day to day. His motto seems to be "Just do it!" You will never know what he truly thinks and he will never tell you his real feelings for you. These characteristics sound similar to those of the of the Pit Bull man, with the exception that the Doberman man may never get caught … EVER!

The only time a Doberman might give a second thought to his actions and the hurt they cause is if his maneuvers are discovered. The reason I used the word discovered is because there is a whole realm of undiscovered events taking place behind your back with this guy. The discovery will make you question this person you thought you knew. While you can rant and rage at him about what he's been doing once you've caught him, you might as well face the fact that you may never know about all of his extracurricular activities.

Throughout this "discovery" process, the mistress will stay loyal to your man, hoping he'll tire of your drama so she can finally claim your spot.

The majority of women in relationships with a Doberman man might suspect something fishy's going on, but may never find definitive proof. That dog is just that good at manipulation and covering his tracks. He has mastered the art of keeping you happy to help divert your attention —his above-average money might also help to cover up a multitude of sins for you.

SEX DRIVE

The Doberman must be good in bed to keep two women happy. The problem is, one woman is happier than the other. Guess Who?

THE PIT BULL

*Having kids with the Pit Bull man
is a 50/50 proposition.
He can either calm down a little while
remaining a Pit Bull at heart or he can
leave you with the children while he runs
plumb crazy. Yet, he will love his kids
and will take a bullet for them if necessary
just as any dog would.*

The Pit Bull

Well...this may take a minute due to the fact that many women deal with this type of man or a close replica. The Pit Bull man is that guy who makes you feel really safe when you're with him. He's so safe and possessive that his initial behavior might give you a false sense of security. You might feel so good about things that even if he looks at another woman you think, *"Go ahead and look because I got your heart."* All I can do is laugh at this thinking, because the Pit Bull personality is divided like a pie.

The Pit Bull man can repeat this secure, feel good process with you and many other women — simultaneously. The Pit Bull always has at least one back up woman. It satisfies his insatiable desire to be a conqueror.

He has an excess amount of energy. On an average day a Pit Bull man might go to the gym, play on a team, build things, and satisfy his crazy sex drive. When you see this behavior, you might wonder, *"Can he control himself when I'm not around?"*

The Pit Bull loves to be intimidating, which means anything from growling at other dogs (men) to getting tattoos or taking steroids to increase his intimidation factor. This can be appealing to the woman who loves these types of testosterone-filled displays. The Pit Bull man can go for little spurts without any drama, but you can be sure the calm won't last long.

Just like the dog he is, this man will go out, flirt, and sex every woman he wants. However, if the Pit Bull finds another dog in *his* yard, "LOOK OUT!" The Pit Bull man is jealous with a capital J. His reaction to someone invading his territory will be extreme. This excessive jealous reaction might be misconstrued as territorial or "protecting his woman," which some women find cute. WOW!

Don't get this dog's behavior twisted and think he's in love with you. The Pit Bull has his sights set on dominating another, and he might set them on you just to mark time until he finds the real thing.

If you think you're dating a Pit Bull and want a relationship, you must growl back and you *must not* flinch. From the very beginning you need to show lots of resistance and no signs of weakness. Take the time to mirror his moves, because he doesn't like a true, long-lived challenge. The anger that produces his energy does not allow for a long fight. So, stand firm and be alert because the Pit Bull goes for the jugular. He always aims to win.

If you're involved with a Pit Bull, you've pretty much already been conquered. The best thing to do is put on your protective gear, because the pit bull is not going to allow you to walk away quietly. If you try, all bets are off. In the world of the Pit Bull leaving him means he has to lash out and put you in your place. He will slander you, disrespect you, try to pick fights, and then do everything he can to get you tangled in his web again. His ultimate goal is to start the conquering process all over again. He knows that if you fall into this trap, it can extend his contract with you for an undetermined amount of time.

When you first met this Pit Bull, you probably went against the advice of your family and friends when they told you not to date him because they could see he was a dirty dog. You, on the other hand, saw a man that would take a bullet for you with his teeth, and intimidate ex-boyfriends. Maybe he disliked all your friends, and pointed out everyone's faults, but you overlooked those flaws because you thought the rest of the package was so good.

You went along with his views of your friends and dropped them in favor of him. What this did was play right into his plan of putting you on an island he created so you won't have any support when he starts showing his true colors. Once the Pit Bull gets you on his island, he thinks, *Let the games begin!*

With no support, no rafts, and no one to hear you scream on this island you now call your life, you can only hear is his voice. He continuously mixes lies with the truth to keep you off balance and prevent you from seeing the truth. Your friends just shake their heads because they can see his game as clear as day.

This situation makes you look totally weak and like a prime mark for the Pit Bull's friends, who will try to get with you behind his back! Why, you ask? It's because they've seen how he treats you and how you just take that treatment without a fight. Plus, he may be spilling intimate details of your relationship.

You may still be feeling secure knowing your Pit Bull's intimidation skills and thinking, *His friends know he would kill them if they come on to me.* However, the reason his friends don't feel any real fear is because they have enough ammunition to bury him. They could bring the Pit Bull to his knees, and possibly you along with him. Feel me! A wounded animal is the easiest prey to capture.

SEX DRIVE

The Pit Bull's sex drive is utterly insane. Anything, and I do mean anything, is fair game — in the car, outside and all kinds of dare devil situations. He may even ask you to do things that make you wonder about his sexuality for a split second. The Pit Bull does his best work in the bed after an argument he instigated.

Don't worry. Like anything else in life, the excitement from his mixture of anger and sex will get old for you. When in a relationship with the Pit Bull, sometimes you want the tool without the ignorant MoFo attached to it.

THE JACK RUSSELL

Kids with the Jack Russell man can be great just get ready for matching jerseys.

The Jack Russell

The Jack Russell man is a naturally happy-go-lucky type who will be a devoted, sometimes overly devoted, and loving man. Did I mention love on overdrive? This is the type of man that will give you potential non-cheating, trustworthy, loyal qualities that you may want in a mate — he might even be your super mate, since he's also hardworking, intelligent, diligent, and loves kids.

Sounds ideal, doesn't he? There is just one small problem ... okay, maybe a few small problems. The Jack Russell man is the type who will make you his entire world. He just hasn't mentioned this to you yet! Just like the Jack Russell terrier he has a strong instinct to chase, meaning he can and will hunt you down. He's pretty much sworn you in without you even knowing you took office. Some women fall for this, while others say to themselves, "Slow down, sir, you're moving kind of fast."

The Jack Russell man is usually small in size but doesn't suffer too much from "little big man syndrome." This means he doesn't have to be right all the time and that's a plus. However, all little men come with a different set of pride issues. This particular type of man can keep it covert even after he has sworn you in without your knowledge.

At this point you can pretty much consider yourself in an official relationship. He may not be your boyfriend but as far as he's concerned, you *are* in a relationship. Yes, you are! Some women like this attention and some can't stand it. The Jack Russell man is the type who goes full steam ahead, sometimes without an anchor. Unless you pull the plug on the little man, the shallow waters may begin to deepen quickly, sometimes overnight.

If you give this man an inch, he will take a mile. So, it's better to put the brakes on early in the relationship, i.e. pre-boyfriend stage. Sometimes, if you slow the pace of the Jack Russell man he might just meet your qualifications, with only a few minor imperfections.

He is the guy who will plan your entire day, even if it's your only off day and all you want to do is relax. He is also the type who will call you at work and text you while he's at work. He'll want to meet you for lunch, even though you may go home to him every night or have plans to see each other later that evening. He just can't get enough of you. This will work for a woman who can deal with this type of no space situation. In fact, you and your little man might be a match made in heaven.

If you can't handle wearing matching T-shirts, coordinating outfits, and having planned days, morning talks, texting all day, meeting at lunch and dinner, then the Jack Russell man can work your nerves completely into the ground even though he may be sweet at times. If you are the type of person who requires a certain amount of "me" time, then I suggest you move on quickly because the Jack Russell man is a relentless relationshipper. The more time you take making your decision, the harder you will make it on yourself. Tick-tock!!!!

SEX DRIVE

The Jack Russell man's sex drive is like the little train that said, "I think I can ... I think I can!" He will try his hardest to please you. He may be a C– but you'll give him an A for effort.

THE GREYHOUND

Kids can be quite an adjustment for the Greyhound man. Children can have a funny but positive effect on some men, though it might take a while.

The Greyhound

The Greyhound man is a personality type who is most likely in sales, part of corporate America, or maybe in some aspect of the sports industry. He appears to have a good job, and even if he doesn't he definitely has the appearance of affluence down to a science.

The Greyhound man does a substantial amount of traveling due to his job or business ventures. It will seem like he is always on the go. Even when he is at home, there will be some urgent thing that has to get done or some pressing unfinished business on his agenda.

He is also the man who has a life of his own that is interesting yet personal. He may be on the down low and may be wiling to try anything sexual at least once. He could also pay for an escort, be addicted to porn, be a chronic masturbator, alcoholic, etc. — the list can go on and on.

The Greyhound man has spent a lot of time alone so he takes his privacy seriously. One thing is definitely for sure; he will never tell on him.

True Greyhound men are organized individuals who can also be brave, devoted, laid-back, charming, and intelligent. The reason I define them as "true" Greyhounds is because there are imposters out there, but we will get to them later.

If you're interested in a Greyhound man, you'll want the answer to the questions: Is he boyfriend material ... the settling down type ... husband material? The Greyhound man would answer yes to every single one of those questions.

The keys to keeping a Greyhound man interested are:

1. **Respect for what he does in his career.** Going after challenges in his job allows the Greyhound to be a Greyhound, just like a canine greyhound's instincts are to run down prey. So, don't downplay the importance of his job.

2. **The Greyhound man does not like to be interrogated;** it takes his mind off business and makes him feel off balance. So, this is a serious no-no for him, even if he does not say anything about it initially.

3. **You must also trust him,** even if you have to seem oblivious to the possible enticements life may present to your Greyhound when he's away on business. You must be willing to live by the philosophy that what you don't know really doesn't hurt you!

4. **The Greyhound's woman must have a life of her own,** but she must accept that no plans can be made without a brief consultation with her Greyhound, because he has a life too. If you fail to do this, you might find that he's already booked.

5. **The woman must be able to surprise him** with some accomplishments of her and experiences of her own. The Greyhound man is willing to listen and contrast his experiences with hers. This may really open him up.

The Greyhound man despises a phony woman who sees him only as a great catch and isn't willing to go the extra mile for him. This woman will find herself drastically unprepared for a relationship with a Greyhound man. He will see right through this type of female and take note of her disorganization, messy living quarters, trash-filled car and sloppy wardrobe. He's no dummy. This woman might qualify for casual sex with him, but not a relationship.

If you are in a relationship with the Greyhound man you may find yourself alone much of the time, with a close watch on the calendar planning the next sighting of your man. Don't let this discourage you. For a chosen few this may be just what the doctor ordered. This time allows you some "me" time, thinking time, and most importantly time to miss your Greyhound. Ironically, the more time you spend in a relationship with him the more you might want him to go off again so you can enjoy more "me" time.

If you're needy, clingy, and suffer from codependency, however, he won't be the man for you. You will either go back to the drawing board or you'll spend a lot of time pretending like you like this style of relationship.

SEX DRIVE

The Greyhound man's sex drive can seem great due to the length of time between each episode. He may throw in something out of the ordinary because he is well-traveled and has had non-traditional experiences.

THE SAINT BERNARD

Kids with the Saint Bernard man can be cool. He is a good dad — but a lazy one. Also, be prepared for the Saint Bernard's attempt to make his child live the dreams he stopped chasing.

The Saint Bernard

The Saint Bernard man is often mistaken for a German Shepherd man, they have many of the same traits. The difference is the Saint Bernard man is lazy and on the chunky side. He is the type who's home eighty-five percent of the time if he's not working.

He's an avid sports lover but he isn't going to the park with any kind of ball. He may be a great cook or involved with someone who is great in the kitchen. Television and the computer are his passions. Working-out and a healthy lifestyle are not in his daily, weekly or monthly regimen. He is good at watching the kids but not really watching them.

The Saint Bernard man's friends are just as lazy as he is. They probably have a ritual of getting together to watch football and talk, either reflecting on when they played a sport and almost made it or reminiscing about someone they knew who almost made it. The

Saint Bernard man is critical of real athletes, voicing complaints like "They could've made that catch with the game on the line!" or "How could he make that error with a few seconds to go in the fourth quarter?"

Like their dog counterparts, the Saint Bernard's size makes them look a bit intimidating and when you're out with him he can even put his game face on. You know deep down inside he's a true Pudding Pop, but it doesn't matter to you because most of the time his little deception works.

Some women love that they know where they'll find their Saint Bernard nearly 99 percent of the time. It makes them feel secure. They'll deal with a little laziness, excess alcohol, not working out, and his doing a so-so job on chores around the house — they think it's a good trade-off for the security.

What you might not know is the Saint Bernard man admires the Pit Bull man and all other roguish dogs. They love to hear stories about these guys and their other women. He might act the same way, if only he had the energy and charm to pull it off. Since he doesn't, he soaks in their stories in like a sponge. The dead give-away to his little secret fascination with the rogue lifestyle may be his porn collection, or his porn-filled browser history. He may love the drama the Internet can bring to him while he sits in his La-Z-Boy. Other issues can be swinging, dating, porn, match-making, MySpace and Facebook for reunions with past ghosts.

Women in relationships with Saint Bernards aren't bothered by the fact that not too many other women gawk at their Big Lugs. They're also not bothered by the fact that he masturbates on a regular basis. "It's just him," they say. But for every time you've caught him in the act you need multiply that times ten. Now you say, "Houston we have a problem!"

As I mentioned earlier, the Saint Bernard man is usually at home and almost always on your radar so most of his little antics go unrecognized. Deep down most women who settle with a Saint Bernard man really aren't bothered by their guy's many small problems. The reason is he doesn't give them too many headaches compared to what goes on with their friends and coworkers' men. The Saint Bernard's woman is confident and knows that "he isn't going anywhere."

The words most associated with the Saint Bernard man are comfort and convenience. Even if he's caught doing something you don't like, who else is going to deal with his mess? He's what you call a "customized" man and your life together has too many variables and rituals to put the big man out. Some of those rituals could be watching favorite TV shows, watching sports, and don't forget about the few times he popped in one of his special DVD's to get your opinion and reaction.

The Saint Bernard is not a natural cheater mainly because of these traits:

- **His appearance.** He is not the best dressed and grooming is an option for him, not a necessity.

- **His "special" charm**. It takes a specific kind of woman to like this type of man.

- **His energy, or lack of it.** He doesn't have the energy to go out and look for trouble, plus he likes to stay near his home base. So, if for some strange reason he does do a little fooling around it's probably with one of your friend, somebody in the neighborhood, or the wife or girlfriend of one of his friends. Isn't that something? He's not going out looking for trouble but if something comes into his territory, he may or may not take a crack at it.

SEX DRIVE

The Saint Bernard's sex drive is similar to the German Shepherd's — they both like the same ole same ole. This may not be a bad thing in most cases. The only difference between him and the German Shepherd man is that he might've watched a movie or heard a story that makes him want to try something new. So, the Saint Bernard may surprise you some nights by making the experience slightly different. He may start off strong but will finish in his same old way. Just like in football, when in doubt go to the bread and butter play.

THE CHIHUAHUA

Kids with the Chihuahua man can be a military-style family situation. Unless he becomes overwhelmed with something else, he will find it difficult to let you have any power. Overall, he will do his best to be all he can be with the kids.

The Chihuahua

The Chihuahua man is small in size but huge in ego. He is a real piece of work and suffers from all the symptoms of little/big man syndrome, including overcompensation and overreaction to minor situations. This little sucker can blow anything out of proportion, from meaningless arguments with you and the kids to altercations with others when you guys are out on the town.

He will do anything he thinks will gain him respect or defend his pride. That's why most little men like plus-sized women or a woman with a few self-esteem issues, since they seem to be more willing to deal with his often obnoxious behavior and random temper tantrums.

The Chihuahua man can be controlling and angry at times. You would not want this little runt as your boss! He could make your job a living hell if you're not one his favorites.

In a relationship, he counters this nasty behavior with sweetness and generosity to help keep you happy. He may seem to have a hard shell in public, but can be Silly Putty in his woman's hands. He can be aggressive and loving at the same time.

His main problem is that he can never get over his small size, and sometimes tries too hard to overcome his perceived shortcomings. His "little engine that could — I got this" mentality can be somewhat attractive to a woman who doesn't mind a pocket-sized man with a little temper.

In the beginning of a relationship, the Chihuahua man will do just about anything to prove his value to you — work hard, play hard, and sex hard. This is how the Chihuahua operates. He wants to get your attention and prove that he can be more valuable than a big man.

Unless size really matters to you, the Chihuahua man can be a nice little catch. He can be a hard worker and a good provider. He's also great at doing chores around the house such as gardening, cutting the grass, painting, and repairing little things. He is handy on the computer and probably frequents the gym.

This little sucker has a lot of steam to let off, for some reason. If he doesn't vent it in some shape, form or fashion, he could wind up taking it out on you in the form of a meaningless argument. The Chihuahua man can also be emotional at times.

This can be a good relationship as long as you don't cross the line. That means never, ever do the following:

- Step on his pride
- Stare at another man when you're out together
- Joke about the sexiness of another man, even if the guy is on TV
- Argue with him in public
- Criticize him in front of his friends
- Do anything that can hurt the little man's feelings

Even though he may be small in size, the Chihuahua man can make you feel somewhat secure because he won't back down. He talks a good game, telling you how he had to either put someone in his place or almost kicked someone's butt. You take these stories with a grain of salt, knowing how he likes to make himself appear larger than life.

This little man's motto is "do it big!" ... well, as big as he *can* do it, anyway. Overcompensation is the name of his game. The Chihuahua man never forgets his small size and is always trying to prove how big he really is.

Even when he's not trying to compensate, the "little/big man syndrome" just seems to seep out of him. He has to be the king, guru, and the final authority on everything. Trust me! Even if that it's totally meaningless, he will have the last word on it, no matter what.

He's the type of man who runs his household like a dictatorship with the illusion of democracy. Some women need this, but if you don't go for that type of thing, the Chihuahua man is not for you.

Just remember, the Chihuahua is all bark with a little bite. So, if you can tolerate a little man who feels a lot of pressure to act big, you should be okay. Just be prepared to walk on eggshells around his ego from time to time.

SEX DRIVE

The Chihuahua man's sex drive is going to be whatever he thinks a big man does to get the job done. Yes, little/big man syndrome affects everything. This means the little man will try to bring the same amount of pressure or even a little more than a big guy would. The need for overcompensation can also explain why he goes overboard in this area. To sum it up, he can surprise you sometimes and other times it will be just what you expected!

THE GREAT DANE

Kids with the Great Dane man can be all right but in case of an emergency, be prepared to hold it down.
Overall, the Great Dane man love kids and can be a great father.

The Great Dane

The Great Dane man is a gentle giant. He's probably an athlete or an ex-athlete. Having a tall man tends to give women an automatic sense of security and can give a boost in confidence they might be lacking.

The Great Dane is a laid-back man of few words. He is so laid back that he's probably only a click away from being lazy. Since the Great Dane man has been an athlete most of his life, it's hard for him to get back in the real world after the pampered lifestyle the world of sports offered him.

Let me explain. When he was an athlete, people indulged him and let him slide — from his time in college all the way to the pros. He's used to getting all sorts of passes and special treatment from teachers, professors, alumni and fans. Reality hits hard once those perks are gone.

Because of their sports backgrounds, Great Danes often are used to handouts when it comes to qualifications need for jobs and doing real work. Many times they were given grades they didn't deserve, jobs they didn't work and all sorts of other perks, just because they were athletes. Being used to this treatment might cause them problems when it comes to employment and a good work ethic after they leave sports behind, unless they were smart enough to use sports networking opportunities that presented themselves during their glory days.

For the Great Danes who didn't take advantage of these opportunities, life can be a serious adjustment. It can mean you end up with a different Great Dane than what you started with.

Let me explain the differences. You may start out with a tall, athletic man of stature with a fat bank account. This may also mean big tools, big toys for them to play with and a man that other women can look up to. Other men think twice about testing this Great Dane.

This man's money, vehicle, status, and reputation can be attractive, tempting and appealing to a multitude of women who are looking for a "savior" to take them away. Negative! If money is your God, you will be a slave to it.

All of this can cause this Great Dane man to get a lot of female attention. His main girl must be strong enough to know this will happen and that he loves to be social. She must have a swag that says, "I got him and he ain't going nowhere."

On the other end of the coin is the second type of Great Dane. This is the guy who didn't see the writing on the wall and take advantage of those same opportunities before he became a has-been. He becomes the man who is always trying to get back to his glory days by working out and still holding on to the dream, even though the dream has long since passed him by. Nevertheless, he has the nerve to lazily stroll around with the swagger of an accomplished Great Dane.

His fervor to re-enter the lifestyle may last for a few years. You might also think he can really make it back to the big leagues, and keep holding onto the dream tighter than he does. Most times, he even has his family and friends convinced he'll make it, to strengthen his cause.

You will finally come to the realization that these damn dreams aren't ever coming true, and that the tryouts and personal trainers aren't paying the bills. He's not even making any progress. That's when those jogging pants, basketball shorts, and flip-flops might start to turn your stomach. Especially if all of this dream chasing means he can't hold down a stable job because he's always trying out for teams and working out.

Not making a change at this point can spell disaster. If this type of Great Dane man doesn't get it together and go get a career already, he might find himself minus his woman. Don't give up, ladies, there is always hope! Find a way to get your man motivated and moving on to something other than sports.

SEX DRIVE

The Great Dane man's sex drive can be as big as he is or maybe not quite what you expected. Big things don't always come in tall packages. Sometimes he may possess a hero in half a shell. The Great Dane's stamina in bed isn't always what you thought he ought to have. As the old saying goes, "The bigger they are the harder they fall." Really!

LABRADOR RETRIEVER

Kids with the Labrador man can be great because he's the type who gets along well with kids, as long as the children get their strength from their mother.

The Labrador Retriever

It's easy to take advantage of the Labrador Retriever man. All I can say to the women who take advantage of this nice guy is, "You should be ashamed of yourself!"

However, if you aren't taking advantage of your Labrador man then this could be a nice safe place to be. The Labrador will work diligently to get things done. It won't necessarily be done the right way, but no matter what he's going to give it the old college try. This guy will fool you from the outside and you might think he's something he's not until you get to know him.

The Labrador man comes in many colors, shapes, sizes and appearances. You've probably come in contact with, gone to school with or worked with this type of man. He is a hard worker, for sure, especially when he is trying to impress his lady. He is dedicated to keeping his lady happy and always puts himself second in every situation — to the point where he may seem a bit brainless at times.

Because of this drive to impress and please his lady, the Labrador man is vulnerable when pursuing the lady in his sights or when he's in a new relationship. Many women use these men for what they can get, because it's like "taking candy from a baby."

Ladies all know this guy. You can get him to do almost anything as long as you show him a little interest in return. Heck, even if you show no interest at all, he's still going to go for broke and try to make you his girl — buying you lunch, giving you minor loans if he knows you need the money, etc. He might even secretly pay a bill or two for you. He's also the type who will eagerly be ready to move in shortly after your first date.

This guy will take whatever abuse you deal him, including hanging up on him, cussing him out, belittling him in front of friends, etc. He might even tolerate a little physical abuse. Some women can deal with this, but most women, especially ones who are strong and aggressive, can only take it for a short time because the potential to take advantage of him is just too great.

The Labrador is a good guy. He will look to strong men for advice on his relationships and other matters on a regular basis. His one itty-bitty problem is that he doesn't listen to any of the advice.

If his relationship situation starts to worsen, the Labrador man feels exposed. Some mistake his kindness for weakness and view him as a weak man. The more abuse his woman dishes out to him, the more he just keeps coming back for more. Isn't that amazing?

Most women don't intend for the relationship to go this direction but somehow, it does. Some women don't have an off switch and will keep erasing the line the Labrador man has drawn in the sand to see if he will ever say no or walk away. Surprisingly, he never does.

He may offer a little resistance but you can see through it; he is transparent. You can just kick him in the bootie and he'll come right back like a boomerang!

As this relationship goes on, it gets frustrating. Cheating becomes an outlet for bored for ladies dealing with this type of man. The woman may find the relationship so boring that she doesn't even care if she gets caught — subconsciously she *wants* to get caught. If cheating isn't her thing but she's sick of the boredom, the thought of leaving him will cross her mind every day.

Don't get it twisted, the Labrador man is thinking the same thing times ten; he just doesn't have the nards to leave. Instead, he waits to be taken away by another woman. So, ladies, be very careful when you consistently mismanage your Lab; it can mean the joke is on you in the end.

The "other woman" has seen how you've mistreated your Labrador man and may decide to do something about it. She might not want him for herself but would love to release him from your grasp. Just as an animal rescuer or a dogcatcher rescues mistreated animals, she "rescue" your man and will either keep him or play catch and release. Either way, the mission is complete and you're out of the picture.

To your surprise, his "rescuer" may be one of your friends or one of his coworkers. The abuse that you dished out, possibly unintentionally, will be the beginning of your own demise. You had the delusion that he would just take whatever you threw at him and still stay by your side.

Because he was so willing to please you and take all the abuse, you start to think all men are this way. You may not mind losing your Labrador man because you think the next man will tolerate the same sorry treatment from you. The joke is on you. Not only have you lost your Labrador to another woman but you've gained nothing in return. The days of your man kissing up to you even when you were dead wrong are over because your Labrador man is gone.

You may cover this loss by saying, "I'm glad he's gone!" "He wasn't my type anyway" or "I wanted a man instead of a doormat." All of these clichés are covering the fact that you're actually thinking, *"Damnnnnnn, I screwed up!"*

The outcome could've been different if you'd treated your man with a little respect and had not taken advantage of him all the time. It's back to the drawing board time for some and blissful misery for others.

The Lab has a soul mate out there, he just takes a beating while trying to find her. There are no guarantees he'll find "The One" but he'll be the guy who's always out there trying anyway.

SEX DRIVE

The Labrador man's sex drive is whatever yours is. Even though you don't thoroughly respect him in all capacities, the sex can be good, great, or just plain protocol. The way you feel will dictate what goes on and will make or break the level of intensity with sex. (Even though that's true for almost all women.)

THE POODLE

Kids with a Poodle man can be good because Poodles get along well with kids. It may take him time to adjust to the new lifestyle and sharing may be an experience.

13

The Poodle

The Poodle man is highly intelligent, easy to train, and skillful. He has many great qualities, but also has as many mood swings as a pregnant woman in her third trimester. This is not the only characteristic that separates the Poodle man from other men.

The Poodle man can be very well kept. Anything that lets him pamper himself is something the Poodle thinks he deserves. You won't have to introduce him to manicures, pedicures or standing appointments at the barber. He'll also indulge in all sorts of dainty things and "beauty treatments" the ordinary man might not even consider. This guy is all about anything that has to do with him.

The Poodle man is also the type who won't budge when he's set his mind on something for himself. He can be so fussy and bitchy that it sometimes makes you wonder if his metrosexual act is really hiding an undercover homosexual or better yet a bisexual prefer-ence. All the signs are there but there's no evidence.

Nevertheless, always remember what goes on in the dark usu-ally comes to light. So, there is no need to think too hard on it. All you can really do is play the hand you're dealt. Never go searching for dirt on your Poodle man because you're sure to find something you don't like.

If you're involved with a Poodle man and you question his sex-uality; you're probably right. You might wonder why you didn't see it earlier.

Most Poodle men have better than average jobs in order to sup-port their grandiose, self-centered lifestyle. Some Poodles, though, will allow themselves to be "kept" men if they can find ladies who are willing to keep them in the manner they deem "necessary." How about that!

It may be a turn-on for some women to have a man who is neat as a pin, possesses exceptional dressing skills, and is extremely well groomed. Women that love competition enjoy the fact that the Poodle man is often a little eye candy for other women.

The catch is that you must have similar interests and be very organized in order to stay in the Poodle man's orbit. If not, he will start to nitpick you and the relationship. In his mind, he really does *not* need you!

In reality, this is not true. Even the Poodle needs a compliment just like every other man. So, if you're involved in a relationship with a Poodle man you have to play the role of a partner with the hint of relationship.

SEX DRIVE

A Poodle man is highly intelligent, so he will figure out a way to satisfy you. You can be sure it won't be a boring ordeal! Since he has feminine characteristics and is a certified metrosexual, he may try some questionable moves in bed. These moves will make you go "hmmmm..." But, what the heck ... he says he's not gay.

THE MUTT

Kids with the Mutt man can go either way, depending on a few variables. In this situation, the kids can cause the Mutt man to transform into the dog he truly wants to be. This is why it can be either good or bad. If the Mutt man has established himself, he can be as great as any father can be. If he has not, the fatherhood experience can be just as confusing and frustrating as his actions. Remember, all dogs have potential to be great fathers.

The Mutt

The Mutt breed has a larger population than most. The reason for this is these men don't really fit into any specific category. The Mutt man's moves are fluid — and tend to fit what he's feeling at the moment.

The Mutt man is the type who exhibits the qualities of many different dogs because he may be truly confused about how to conduct himself and who he really is. He might continuously try different methods to solve his problems and get things done. He might also try new sexual experiences and mix things up in his relationships. The Mutt man does this even if things are going relatively well for him.

Some men become the Mutt to fight the inner dog they really are. Most Mutts can do a great job of disguising the fact that they don't know who they are until they either figure it out or get stuck as the dog life dictates.

An example of this is the party animal jock who is a little quick tempered, extra flirtatious, and has a problem with being monogamous, like a Pit Bull. He keeps his party animal mentality, but after two or more kids, a couple of extra pounds, and a job he's not thoroughly happy with, he has no choice but to become a Saint Bernard. He gives up the other persona and resigns himself to sitting around the house watching football, baseball, basketball or whatever on TV. It's not that he doesn't still want to be a Pit Bull, he's just in too deep at this point to be anything other than a Saint Bernard.

This is only one example. The combinations can go an infinite number of ways, depending on job status, financial situation and other components of the man's life.

The Mutt man is the sort who appears to have one major characteristic of one breed and the minor characteristics of many others. Deep down, he is truly only one breed, but doesn't have the conviction to just be it. If you pay close attention, you'll see this dog from time to time and can bring him to the surface. This trait can be good for some relationships, but may be like a trip through hell for others.

Most men find themselves in Mutt mode at some point in their lives. There's no specific time when this happens — it could be at the beginning of adolescence or it could wait to show itself until his mid-life crisis.

Many young Mutts are motivated by friends, trends, music, and TV icons. They are desperately searching for an identity and are confused about who to be and how to act. This is normal, since being a Mutt is synonymous with immaturity. Young Mutts try to fill this void with pants sagging to the ground, outlandish hairstyles and mimicking favorite celebrities, i.e. if his favorite musician is rocking skinny jeans then he's rocking them as well. While aspiring to celebrity isn't a bad thing, getting lost in another person's identity can cause a whole new set of issues.

This mimicking bleeds over to the Mutt's behavior as well. A young Mutt might decide he should mirror his favorite bad boy star's conduct, which can be detrimental if he can't eventually figure out who he really is and act accordingly. If he doesn't grow out of this immaturity, the Mutt might not attain a solid future because he will never be able to establish the true priorities of his life.

If the young Mutt is involved with a mature dog, no matter which breed, he can make it through the Mutt period in his life and come out good on the other side. If he imprints on the mature dog and mimics his good behavior, he will rearrange some things in his life and remove the confusion.

The Mutt who waits until later in life to make changes, may experience confusion mixed with indecisiveness. This could be considered his "mid-life crisis" because he picks up the traits of many dogs and tries them out until he finds his new true self. This transition period can be critical for a mature Mutt because he can either snap out of it or get stuck and be an immature Mutt for the rest of his life.

SEX DRIVE

The Mutt man's sex drive is just as mixed up as he is. You just never know what prize you may pull out of his Cracker Jack box — you could be in for something great or just a great disappointment. Usually, if he talks a good game you can expect the exact opposite. His performance depends on his motivation and possibly a little help from one of those magical pills.

All Men *Are* Dogs — Make Them Behave!

The pursuit of happiness, when connected to a relationship, can lead to an obstacle course with untamed twists, turns, loops and challenges. Your goal to achieve said happiness should be a healthy lifestyle connected to a healthy relationship — and the key to a healthy relationship starts with you.

For example, a man may want to be in a relationship with the first beautiful woman he sees. That relationship could be one of friendship or it could be intimate. It is usually up to the woman to decide which of these it will be, since she has the final authority, while the man, a natural-born hunter, does exactly what he is born to do — hunt.

The woman's authority does have a limited scope. Usually, once intimacy is involved, she has lost most of it. Women equate intimacy with bonding. This usually brings about an uncontrollable emotional instinct that blinds her and causes her common sense to take a hike.

The emotional instinct linked to intimacy makes most women second-guess their true feelings for the man. This is made worse if the sexual experience was exceptionally good for the woman. Intellectually, she may know the guy is not really her type and isn't a good fit for a long, healthy relationship but her emotions override her brain. So, she continues to have intimate encounters with this man and starts redesigning her future to fit him into it.

This man might be a cheater, gambler, drug addict, and smoker. He might have no ambition, no drive, and be a verbal or physical abuser. None of this matters to the woman because the intimacy blinders are in place and she has been dickmatized!

Because she is so enthralled with this man, a swift, no harm/no foul exit is nearly impossible. This semi-relationship can drag on for quite some time if she doesn't decide to make a move. Finally, she must cut out the intimacy or completely eliminate him from her life so she can move on.

To do this, she has to wake up and plot her escape. This probably won't be easy because she has a history with this man who should have had only one page in the book of her life. When her eyes are finally open, she'll think, *If only I could've left him out of my life.*

If her time with this man led to a child, then she can never completely sever her relationship with him. She is truly stuck, and will have to deal with him for many years to come.

This is why a healthy relationship should be every woman's goal. This means finding a person who balances your well-being and has all the traits you admire. Having a relationship with someone who impacts your life in a positive way can bring about happiness and even help you live longer. While being in an unhealthy relationship can be mentally, physically and emotionally draining and will ultimately bring you down. It's like asking the bartender for a shot of poison on the rocks.

While a dog is said to be man's best friend, a man/dog can also be woman's best friend. It all depends on the dog she selects and the boundaries she sets initially. A man will only go as far as he is allowed, so the woman needs to take the initiative and structure the relationship from the beginning. It's all on you, ladies — men are just along for the ride while they're trying to decide how to get in.

We can always look back at a situation and say, "I can't believe I dealt with that mess!" or "What was I thinking?" This is the beauty of learning a lesson from life experiences. My advice is to start knowing beforehand. This takes careful observation and patient decision-making.

Warning — If intimacy is the foundation of your relationship then get ready for the house to fall down. It may take a few days or a few years but just like a house built on sand, it is sure to fall down.

When you're exerting your final authority, keep in mind how badly intimacy can cloud your judgment. You should seriously consider building the relationship without the intimacy. This allows you to really get to know the man you've chosen without those pesky emotional blinders coming down over your common sense. Doing this will make his true nature expose itself quickly.

Ladies, I'll say it again. It's better to delay your gratification, since it could mean the difference between ending up with Mr. Right and being stuck with Mr. Right Now.

Straying

First off, I must clarify the meaning of straying. What I mean is being unfaithful to you, his woman. Straying can come in many forms, and technology has opened up a whole new avenue of straying possibilities.

In the "good old days," you could be pretty sure your spouse or husband wasn't communicating regularly with someone you didn't know about. Then came the pager and eventually the cell phone with texting/sexting and that surety was suddenly gone. The final blow to your security was combination of the home computer and the internet. Now, your man can stray virtually while he's sitting at home in his La-Z-Boy, possibly with you in the same room!

All of this technology also brought with it more opportunities to stray. He can now meet people he might not have had access to before through email, free porn, instant messaging and chat rooms. Some consider this form of meeting/communicating cheating.

Now you not only have to worry about where your guy is going, you have to wonder what he's doing online and possibly who he's meeting there.

Your man may consider his chats or texting with another woman an innocent friendship, but if he's in a monogamous relationship, what he's doing could be considered a sort of straying from his relationship. Whether it is truly cheating or not, it can cause you anxiety and emotional pain.

This form of straying, if it has gone no farther than talking can probably be disciplined and then forgiven. Yes, I said it — forgiven. If you discover this type of thing going on in your relationship, you should first look at yourself and evaluate how well you've been treating your dog-man. Even though he's done something wrong, there had to be a reason why he was drawn to do it. In other words, there are two of you in the relationship and you both had something to do with the straying and you both have to work it out.

Clarity and communication are key to finding the "what" and "why" behind the straying. This doesn't really mean the details of the straying — you may never know those and probably don't want to. The why is probably that your dog was missing something in his relationship with you and went elsewhere to find it. You just need to figure out what.

Knowing your man's type of dog will help you to evaluate this missing factor — he might not even know exactly what it is. By communicating, you will find clarity and the missing what. Once you know what is, you can decide if you can provide it.

Communication is the master key to your relationship. If the communication breaks down so does everything else. We've all seen relationships that are so fragile it seems like there's nothing but a toothpick holding them together. If you can't tell each other what you want and need and truly listen, then the relationship is doomed to fail.

If you know your dog needs lots of praise and attention but you've been too busy with other things to provide it, then you've ignored his basic need. (He could make the same mistake with you.) If neither of you communicate, the dissatisfaction will build until straying seems the only way to make things better.

Knowing which type of dog your man is can give you valuable insight into exactly what makes him tick. It is imperative to try to understand your dog's needs and see that they're met if you want to continue the relationship. Arming yourself with this knowledge will help to keep you from being blind-sided by straying.

You must also understand the outside elements your dog faces because there are temptations and stressors everywhere that can possibly cloud your dog's judgment. With regular mutual communication, observation and insight you can get through these relationship obstacles and come out with a stronger union.

It's possible that the urge to stray is built into your dog's personality. Like I mentioned earlier, don't get mad at your dog -man for being exactly who he is. If he's inclined to look for excitement, make sure you're the one providing it and he won't look elsewhere.

If, on the other had, you evaluate the situation and find it's not salvageable then it's time to do some serious thinking. Sometimes people's wants and needs change and there's no way to make the old relationship work with these new differences. Or, if the straying transgression is severe and you cannot find a way to trust your dog again, then you might need to go to extreme measures. As the old cliché goes "the more things change the more they stay the same." Whatever the case, only you can decide what's right for you.

STRAYING FROM THE DOG'S POINT OF VIEW

In my opinion, there are three stages to straying. I call them the 3Ps. These stages are useful when determining the difference between straying and flat out cheating. The 3Ps are: peeping, pleasure, and promotion.

Peeping — This is when a guy directly or indirectly flirts to see if he can gain attention. An example of peeping might be flirting with a coworker or someone he comes in contact with on a regular basis just to see if she finds him attractive. Another example is getting a woman's number but never calling it.

This type of activity calls to the hunter in every man. It gives him the thrill of the chase and lets him know he's still got it. This might be as far as the dog is willing to take things, depending on the degree of discipline he possesses. This type of validation might be enough of an ego stroke to satisfy what's missing in his relationship, but other dogs may get caught up in the chase and take it to the next stage.

Pleasure — This may sound totally sexual in nature, but pleasure can be derived in many different forms, including emotional, financial, social, etc. Pleasure comes from intimacy of any kind. The pleasure stage is like being in a speeding car right before it goes over the cliff. Deep down inside he knows he should stop but he's just enjoying it too much. He enjoys the joy ride but doesn't want to face the consequences if he's caught. The test will be whether he puts on the brakes or keeps going until he flies off the cliff.

Promotion — The promotion stage is where you end up when the pleasure vehicle flies off that cliff. Most men can stop at the pleasure stage because they never intend for things to get serious. Some men, however, cannot pry themselves away from the pleasure because they like it better than what they have at home.(This means he's getting something he feels he needs, and he's not getting it from you.)

If things have progressed to this stage, your dog has decided he wants a new home. He either wants to replace you, the woman he has, with a new refreshing experience or he plans on trying to keep you both. No matter what, he plans to get what he thinks he needs. In essence, he has started to view the extracurricular situation as a better fit than what he has, which means he wants to move you to the number-two position in line-up and is anxiously awaiting that move. The promotion stage may not include marriage but it does include a new focus.

This progression through the 3Ps didn't happen overnight. If you had maintained constant positive communication and observation, you and he wouldn't have reached this point. Understanding your mate and all his various angles, will help you this situation.

When I tell you to communicate and observe, this is by no means telling you to snoop around, set him up or try to test him. This type of behavior will only tell him you don't trust him, and it takes a level of trust to engage in any relationship. This trust should be earned by his behavior and actions.

If your dog does something to make you distrust him, don't be so closed that you won't let him regain that trust. It will take work on his part along with sincerity and action. The work involved should be determined by his previous actions and how much you distrust him.

If you find that there is no way you can ever regain the trust you've lost, then it's time to evaluate and consider your options. I would never specifically tell you to leave your mate. That decision is entirely personal and completely up to you.

You're the only one who has to deal with your dog's poop. So, don't let anyone try to define your happiness or make your decisions for you. You have to live with what you decide — good or bad.

Straying Tendencies
by Breed

THE GERMAN SHEPHERD

If your German Shepherd man goes astray — from entertaining another to outright cheating — remember the origin of the breed. Everything and anything is subject to change. Factors such as drugs, alcohol and overall level of resistance can come into play. Hey, Pressure can burst a pipe on many different levels.

Remember ladies: the enemy is not your dog-man. The enemy is an outside element — another dog-less woman and all the temptations she represents. She will try her best to lure your dog into her world. You know how tenacious a woman can be when she wants something. Think about that for a minute and you'll start to see what you're up against!

These dog-less and sometimes unhappy dog owners are driven, uninhibited and will stop at nothing to get the desired results. So, it's as simple as this: the more appealing the man — looks, brains, charisma, stature, hygiene, swagger etc. — the more your man looks a prize to others.

Even though your German Shepherd doesn't have a tendency to stray, he can still fall victim to it under the right circumstances. The German Shepherd is a good, hard working man who lives a routine lifestyle, so if he strays the key element to redeeming the relationship will be how ingrained the other woman has become in his lifestyle.

You'll need to ask how long has it been going on? Does the other woman know about me? Does she know about the kids? If the answer is yes to these questions then you may have a problem.

At this point, your ability to communicate will come into play. If you have a solid foundation, where you built a friendship with your dog before you built the relationship, then you can probably work through it. You're more deeply imbedded in his life than any "other woman" could ever be.

The German Shepherd is loyal by nature unless neglected by his owner. If neglected, he can potentially wander just like any other breed. The German Shepherd does not want to upset his home life, so if you've been good to him but he happens to stray, don't panic. The German Shepherd wears the Loyalty badge with honor.

THE ROTTWEILER

If your Rottweiler man strays, don't mistake him for a German Shepherd. There's a method behind his madness. Remember, he's an even-tempered, loyal and fiercely protective man, but he hates to be confined to the backyard or a kennel.

As a mate, you should interpret these traits to mean he needs to be kept stimulated in many areas — from mental to physical. If your Rottweiler man strays, you must be in a position to ask him for the honest answer as to why. Knowing the reasoning behind his extracurricular activity will help you find the missing elements in your relationship. Once you know what needs fixed, you can be the one to satisfy whatever itches he may need scratched.

The Rottweiler man likes eye candy — like most dogs — but that doesn't mean he'll do more than look, even if given the opportunity. If you come at him with your A-game and give him his own eye candy, i.e. you, then it will make him think twice before entering "other woman" territory.

This guy is a smart dog and won't act unless prompted by lackluster ownership or previous abuse of pride. Good communication is a key component with this breed, because if he does decide to stray it will be strictly for entertainment purposes. The Rottweiler his loves home no matter what.

THE DOBERMAN

If the Doberman man happens to get caught straying, it shouldn't really be a surprise. Remember, the Doberman is a shrewd individual, and he'll be prepared to defend his stance.

What do you do if you think your Doberman has strayed? In many cases, if you accuse him he'll have all his bases covered because he takes care of all the household financial concerns. The combination of financial security and quality time spent with you usually offers him a great alibi. The reason I say alibi is because he is never going to offer any additional information on the allegations.

If you happen to get the telephone number of the other woman and decide to call or if you get the infamous "call from the other woman," be prepared to hear anything — including details that can be a little bone-chilling. You won't necessarily be surprised by the sexual encounters; the surprise will be how brazen his escapades are.

The Doberman man loves his double life, so trying to figure out why he's strayed can be brain-busting and pointless. The Doberman is shrewd and intelligent so he fine ways to disprove the allegations against him no matter what they are. The Doberman has planned ahead for these situations and always chooses women he can manipulate who are more attached to him than he is to them. If the Doberman possesses the Triple S package—Sex, Swag and a Swollen bank account — he can make you want to compromise your boundaries just to keep him. How about that!

By the time the Doberman man finishes poking holes in your allegations and telling you how wrong you are about him, he'll have you convinced you're his number-one concern because he doesn't want to change his home front dynamics. He doesn't want the constant stress associated with that type of change — he wants a speedy recovery from this little bump in the road.

Whatever you decide in this situation, just know that you will need to have the strength to step into the unknown. If you don't, then just take it across the chin and keep things the way they are. At least you're aware that something was going on.

All of this drama might prompt a spike in his generosity to help ease your pain. This behavior trend might be a deal-breaker when it comes to your decision about staying. Think and then do what suites you. If you can take an emotional ass whipping from time to time, keep things the way they. Most women who deal with a Doberman man just turn a blind eye to it all.

PIT BULL

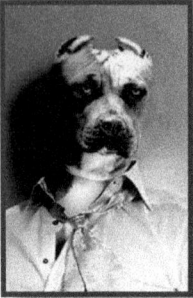

Deep down, you knew your Pit Bull would probably stray based on his previous behavior and tendencies. You were just honestly hoping it wouldn't happen to you. The question is, what do you do?

The answer depends on how your Pit Bull man responds to getting caught. Yep, in this case he'll probably be the one to force your hand. Whether you want to verbalize it or not, you knew what he was. Now, you have to decide if you want to put up with him.

The Pit-Bull man is known for his intimidation and aggression tactics, so if he's caught he can opt to do something you might not be prepared to handle. He'll use this as the ultimate diversion so he can play the "victim" and throw you completely off balance — he's never the victim in any situation.

Don't get me wrong; any dog can use this method as a quick go-to move. However, when used by the Pit Bull it can totally pull the rug out from under you because it's so unexpected. His hope is that keeping you off balance will make his offense seem less severe and give him time to plan his next move.

He will probably turn the tables on you so completely that you'll walk away saying, "What in the world just happened?" What's worse, you left with no closure, no answers, and now you're somehow feeling sorry for *him*. My friend, you have been officially victimized by the Pit Bull.

If indeed happens, it's a huge clue that maybe you should consider taking the next bus out of town. Why, you ask? Because is nothing more than his sneaky tactic to allows him time to regroup and reorganize his operation. The issues will never be truly addressed or solved ... EVER. Since addressing the issues is the first step to fixing things when something like this happens, there's really no need to go further because you can almost guarantee it will happen again.

The other way to approach a straying Pit-Bull can be to put him into a scared straight situation. The success of this approach will depend upon how much he cares for his "bitch" to use dog terms. If he cares deeply for you, he will instinctively do anything to make it right. I mean *anything*. He might even drop to one knee and ask you to marry him. Can you believe some women fall for the "I just got caught so let's get married" trick?

The Pit Bull who cares about you will go to extreme measures to try to keep you, including buying you things, spending more time with you and dropping his other situation immediately to show you that you are his number one woman.

What do you do if this is your Pit Bull's reaction? He hopes that the confusion he's caused will play a role your decision-making process. Don't let it! This time, you need to measure his sincerity and give it some time to determine if you are going back to the same old thing or a semi-changed man.

Remember, the Pit Bull is a possessive individual who does *not* want to imagine you with another guy, let alone see you with one. Reminding him of this can ring a bell and cause the Pit Bull reign it in. If you decide to stick it out and stay with him, tread lightly to be sure he's truly making the effort.

Nevertheless, a Pit Bull is who he is, and since you knew that to start out with you just have to decide what you're willing to put up with. Do what best suits you! If you like the contrast, do it! You are the one who defines your happiness. Hey, it's different strokes for different folks.

A non-Pit Bull owner might wonder why would anyone want this territorial fighter with a propensity for straying. Despite their flaws, a surprising number of women end up with Pit Bulls. It's all about personal preference. Despite what the critics might think, at the end of the day you must do what's best for you. You know and understand what comes with the Pit Bull's territory and so does everyone else, so don't be surprised if there aren't many shoulders to cry on when he does it again.

JACK RUSSELL

If the Jack Russell man decides to get out there, and mix it up a bit and stray, you should be afraid. I say be afraid because if you love all the attention he brings to the table, this extracurricular activity could be hard to swallow. However, if you're on the opposite end of the spectrum, then this might be the excuse you've been looking for.

When the Jack Russell man strays, his woman's feelings are either feast or famine. You either say, "Whew! I needed a little break just to think" or you're crying, "I miss the attention my little Jack Russell gave me."

The Jack Russell is usually the type who strays on impulse. Even though he loves his mate and can be a little over-excited with regard to quality time, he's not bullet proof when it comes to the lure of his female coworkers. Constant flirtatious behavior can break him down, especially if female attention has been lacking throughout his life.

His straying behavior can stem from mismanagement by his owner or from his overall resistance or lack thereof. Don't worry too much, ladies. If he does decide to take a crack at straying in any form, he can be easily found out. He'll find it virtually impossible to keep up consistent lines of communication with more than one woman. I'm not saying it can't be done, but over time it will wear him down. An abrupt change in his behavior and even his attitude could be the first clue to the trouble.

If you catch him, what do you do? Remember that just because the Jack Russell strays doesn't necessarily mean he is out looking for a replacement for you. You should pay attention to the type of attention he was giving the other woman. This will tell you whether you should stay or leave. You should know your Jack Russell well enough to know when he's just playing around or if it's something more serious. With the Jack Russell man, actions really do speak louder than words.

The Jack Russell is known for being a vibrant and loyal dog, but he doesn't like to be teased or hit (physically or verbally). Even though he doesn't truly display the characteristics of little/big man syndrome, his pride is the same size. If he's been treated badly and his pride is bruised, in some cases this can prompt the Jack Russell to act.

THE GREYHOUND

The Greyhound man is a busybody, who can be tempted to do a little straying because of his flexible schedule and long stints away from home. If your Greyhound happens to stray, don't try to figure out where you went wrong.

Remember the type of man you're dealing with and add in a few external factors that can place your dog in the right situation and you might have a recipe for straying. Chances are, if your Greyhound decides to partake it's more the available opportunity than anything to do with you.

The Greyhound man is always on the go and really shouldn't have time to entertain, however, opportunities do present themselves. It's at this point that your man has to decide whether to pursue or ignore. If you're doing what you can as his mate, including keeping up good communication with him, never ending a day on a sour note when he is away, and keeping a non-antagonistic approach to his personal space ... then there's nothing more you can do to help with his decision to not take door number two.

You must remember that Greyhounds do not like a pushover or a woman who's not willing to put her foot down from time to time. The Greyhound also doesn't respond well to harsh discipline. So, if you catch him straying you should remain calm but decisive and firm with your actions.

A true greyhound has drive and intelligence, which are qualities other women find attractive. So, opportunities will keep presenting themselves to him. Ultimately, the decision is on him. If he's happy with his current relationship, the temptation might not be more than a stroke for his ego. If he's dissatisfied, then a-straying he will go.

If do your part and stay on course, your strong bond is not going to be broken easily, no matter what tactics other women employ. The Greyhound who travels for long stints may just be entertaining himself while he's away. If this describes your man, then you'll just have to decide what you're willing to put up with from him.

THE CHIHUAHUA

The little guy has finally done it this time. If your Chihuahua man has managed to slip and engage in a little extracurricular activity — don't panic. Remember, the Chihuahua suffers from little/big man syndrome, which causes him inherent issues and flaws.

The Chihuahua man can be pushed into action or he can just take advantage if a situation presents itself. He usually doesn't get as many shots at this type of action as a big or average-sized man. His jumping at the chance to stray may be a form of overcompensation caused by the dreaded syndrome.

Most Chihuahuas can be mean at times, especially if they control the sticks at home. If your man is not this way, then he probably displays his mini-dominance when he's away from home.

If your Chihuahua man suffers from a severe case of little/big man syndrome, then cheating and other forms of "entertainment" can be expected. The extent to which he lets his syndrome dictate his actions may predict the brazenness of his exploits. This behavior shouldn't come as a total surprise to you — all Chihuahuas have a sneaky side.

Ultimately it depends on how much control and freedom you have allowed your Chihuahua man within your relationship. If you've allowed him total control or he makes the majority of the decisions, then the little guy truly might not care about his actions or getting caught.

On the other hand, if your Chihuahua has a mild temperament and shows minimal signs of little/big man syndrome, this indiscretion might be a case of opportunity seized. He may never admit it, he always feels like he has a point to prove. It just depends on the point.

If someone shows the Chihuahua man additional attention on a consistent basis, they can eventually break him. The Chihuahua doesn't have many opportunities like this and doesn't really know how to act once he's said yes, so the other party in the relationship will define the straying.

In the end, a Chihuahua will be a Chihuahua. No matter how you size it, he is who he is. The Chihuahua man can be a good companion but he's also got a lot of pride, and can be bossy and snappy at times. The key is to not allow your Chihuahua to get away with the things he sees the big dogs doing. Even though he's small, it doesn't make that behavior cute.

THE LABRADOR

Since the Labrador man is usually loyal, this is a tricky one. In most cases, if your dog decides to stray from his home front, you may have caused it. The Lab is gullible and usually can take a lot across the chin from you, but if you put him in a state of vulnerability then he can get side-tracked by a woman who pays attention to him and reassures him.

Even if you don't put any pressure on him, he still might be vulnerable because he can be gullible by nature. Your Labrador man can be a sitting duck if he's on a predator woman's radar. She'll capitalize on his shortcomings. So, you can't blame him for being who he is. Now the question is, what do you do?

It really depends on a couple of variables. One is your mismanagement and lack of respect for your man. You must be careful not to go overboard on the man who seems to let you get away with murder and loves you despite what you've done. Remember, every dog has its day. The funny thing is you won't see it coming if you're not paying attention.

The second and most important thing is your relationship bond. Your Labrador may have previous emotional damage from a past relationship or maybe he has been played a few times and needs a little more reassurance than the average man. If this is true for your Lab, then the bond you create with him can be a form of defense to keep him from straying.

Please remember the Labrador is who he is, so there are never guarantees. If he decides he needs someone to reassure him and it's not you, then he will stray.

THE SAINT BERNARD

If your Saint Bernard man suddenly decides to put himself back in the game, don't be surprised and don't be too alarmed. He's not the type who looks for trouble most of the time, but if trouble falls into his lap he just might do what he's always fantasized about.

This man is a homebody, and doesn't like to go too far outside his territory. So if he does decide to do a little straying, the other woman probably isn't too far away.

What do you do about it? I always ask that question because it's up to you. Remember, the Saint Bernard man doesn't have the energy to keep up the charade for long. He's probably just riding this fun out.

So, if the big lug happens to get caught and doesn't make it right, it can set you back mentally. When deciding what to do, though, you must consider the big picture, whatever that may be.

The bottom line is that he's really not going anywhere. He probably never expected this little "bonus" and just couldn't turn it down. You'd be surprised how loneliness can bring about a vulnerability that can spark fake magic between people.

The Saint Bernard may generally deserve a pass, but that pass depends on your personal tolerance for emotional pain. If he's really sorry, he will spend the rest of his life worrying whether you've paid him back in kind, which is something that can make any dog regret a "good time."

THE POODLE

If your Poodle man decides to do some straying, it might take many forms. The Poodle is attractive to others, so he might suffer from pressure placed upon him by them. He is also the type who might be self-centered, so if he does decide to do anything it's purely because he wants to.

This means there isn't any true form of defense on your part if he decides to get out there. Even though this may be true for any dog, it is most prevalent with the Poodle.

The first thing you must do as a sort of preventive measure is keep your Poodle from getting bored. He is an intelligent dog and gets bored easily if he isn't learning or thinking. Bad things happen when a Poodle man gets bored.

Secondly, and most importantly, is to always stay on top of you're game with your personal appearance. The poodle is the type who likes to stand out in a crowd and having a well-kept lady on his arm plays right into that need.

The Poodle man is a high maintenance alpha dog. It can be a challenge to get him to hunker down because this behavior is in his nature. Breaking him may break you in many ways, but it may be worth it in the end if you are strong and stern.

His straying might come in different forms, from various sources, including clients, coworkers, and friends. The women give him attention and keep his ego stroked. He may even engage in a little bit of sexting through picture mail if some high quality eye candy gives him the right amount of attention. (High quality meaning she is able to pick up the bill and has the beauty to match.)

It's important to remember that Poodles love to be spoiled. Even if he has no intention of taking it to another level, there are women out there who are lonely and thirsty enough to hang around wear your Poodle down. Whether they succeed or not depends on you and the things I mentioned earlier.

Your Poodle man can either handle the pressure or can't deal with it at all. If he's not used to the type of attention he's getting or doesn't have any discipline around the opposite sex, you know what you're dealing with. Once again, it's all up to you.

With the Poodle man, you know you always have to bring your "A-Game" at all times to keep the wolves at bay.

THE GREAT DANE

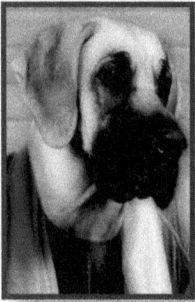

If the Great Dane man wants to get out and stretch his legs, so to speak, and do a little straying he may just be having flashbacks. The Great Dane is usually laid back and chill, but in some cases can do some straying. If you're suspicious, my theory is to look at things from all angles, meaning temptation and opportunity.

The Great Dane man has an automatic presence due to his size, and there is no secret that a lot of women love tall men. If he has good social skills, then he's extra intriguing. If this is your situation, don't be surprised that your man is a target. Always consider the external factors that may set the wheels in motion before he even leaves the door.

If your dog was an athlete, he is thinking he'll get a pass anyway because he's been getting passes throughout his life. Trust that his way of thinking has nothing to do with you. Women love athletes ... men love athletes ... the world loves athletes — that's a lot of adoration, people willing to do what he wants, and temptation. That doesn't make it right, but it is what it is.

Sometimes, it's nothing more than an opportunity presenting itself at a weak moment for your Great Dane. This allows any man without proper discipline and self-control to pull a quick stunt. When a man strays you must know his true dynamics.

Take some preventative measures by doing your part to keep your relationship flowing. The Great Dane is laid back by nature and loves positive reinforcement. If you're in a relationship with him and you're constantly complaining, negative, and under-appreciate him then will literally eat away at the soul of your good-natured guy. This is especially true if it's not followed up with positive reinforcement, which can be something as small as a nice meal or it can be a grand gesture that you know will assure him you love him.

Ultimately what you do about his behavior is in your hands. You can do everything right and things can still go south. That's why in this situation, as well as many others, you must constantly and consistently communicate to understand the mindset of your Great Dane.

THE MUTT

If the Mutt man decides to give in to temptation, it may not be an accident. The severity of the straying will depend on which type of Mutt you're dealing with.

If you are involved in a relationship with a young Mutt who's in the midst of trying to come into his true self, then anything can happen. This whole thing may have all been about curiosity. His sheer fascination with life and the vast number of choices and adventures, combined with peer pressure and whatever else motivates him can combine to make the act of straying seem attractive to him.

This means that if you're with a young Mutt you should probably expect him to do some straying to see if he made a solid choice with you.

There is no true defense mechanism for the young Mutt's actions because he doesn't even know what his next move will be. The only thing you can do to separate yourself from the pack of other females is be loyalty to your dog. He wants you to be down for him no matter what — and I do mean no matter what.

Hopefully, when and if he figures himself out, won't forget your loyalty. I know this sounds like kind of outside the box thinking, but I've met plenty of women who don't mind this role as long as the man comes home to her and doesn't blatantly stray.

On the other side of the spectrum is the mature Mutt man. He might decide to stray because he feels suppressed and wants to try something new to satisfy his curiosity. He may be at the transition period in his life and decide to do some straying to re-prioritize his life. Hopefully you make the cut.

The only defense against a mature Mutt's potential spontaneous action is to stand back and hope he snaps out of. It's really hard to reach someone who doesn't really know his next move, even at a mature age.

What do you do? Well, I can tell you what *not* to do if you're contemplating staying — don't shut down. Shutting down or getting frustrated to the point you keep it all inside can further close the communication lines between you and pretty much signal the beginning of the end.

The settling sets in after the newness starts to wear thin and you're left to work with just the raw material.

Settling

Most females and people in general use this phrase freely and as often as possible when they're single: "I refuse to settle." In reality, you're going to have to settle for some type of irrational behavior someone whose appearance isn't your ideal, because no one is perfect.

So, settle you will ... But to what degree? What are you willing to accept?

Things have a funny way of seeming perfect at the beginning of a relationship. So initially, settling is the last thing on your mind. The settling sets in after the newness starts to wear thin and you're left to work with just the raw material.

You had no clue that his farts would stink so bad, did you? That's funny but in many cases, it is true and it's a problem. Think about it. If he had let one rip on your first date — even if it had squeaked out ... lol — he probably wouldn't have made the roster.

On a more serious note, there are a lot of women in abusive relationships, both verbal and physical in nature. Imagine if your man had hit you on the first date or if he belittled you on your second date. I doubt in either circumstance you would've stuck around for round two.

However, since these little "surprises" took a while to materialize, you might at first think they're a one-time thing. It had to be a mistake and he won't do it again. Even if he doesn't do it again, you're still probably settling. Some women use financial security, children, history, fear of starting over, and a host of excuses to mask settling.

So, settling is not negotiable, it's inevitable.

Training

Women, it's important that you pay close attention to this section even though it's short.

M en do not like to be trained. I repeat men DO NOT like to be trained. Men don't even want to hear a woman claiming to practice in this "witchcraft."

The truth is the process of trying to coexist on any level, from the preliminary to actually living together, is actually a training process. Effective communication is essential because this how both parties establish guidelines and boundaries for the relationship. If you set none, just remember that even a hamster can get out of line.

This training should be fluid, like the Tai Chi. It should be a give-and-take situation with both parties equally represented. That keeps things harmonious and in a state of balance. Therefore, training is an essential a component of any relationship.

The negative connotation comes into play when things are out of balance, i.e. if one person in the relationship tries to dominate. The training I'm talking about here is not really about just what's being done wrong. I'm talking about setting the rules for how you each expect to be treated within the relationship so there are no surprises later on. In other words, "We teach people how to treat us."

So, to all the ladies who say they are "training their man" — be careful with YOUR tactics. The worst thing you can do is suppress the dog — his reaction just might be to turn around and bite you!

Do You Qualify???

When you think about getting a dog, the first thing most people consider is what kind of dog best fits their lifestyle. They think about everything from the dog's aggression, size, temperament and eating habits, to a host of traits the dog may possess. They go through this process to see if this "type" of dog will work for them. This process is called the qualifying stage.

I propose that women should go through the same thought process when looking for a mate, which is obviously a more important decision than choosing a dog. I'm just saying that after you get past the "he's so cute and has pretty eyes" stage, you must start implementing a qualifying stage.

This means that through communication you should be able to gather preliminary information, without interrogating him, to see whether he is worth your time. You should take your time and be thorough; you're choosing a man you intend to spend the rest of your life with. This choice is key to your future personal happiness.

To go back to the dog owner analogy, if a woman works nine hours a day and lives in a one-bedroom studio she should not choose a Great Dane. While it might work for a short time, in the end it's not going to work because it's not a good fit. You can force it and it may work, but one or the other of you will eventually be miserable.

The same goes for dealing with any type of man. You and he must have qualities that mesh if you're going to find the relation-ship you truly want! So, if you love to go out and party, you're going to have to realize that the guy who's a homebody is not right for you — no matter how attractive you find him initially. Neither of you will be able to change who you are, so you'll always be at odds.

That's not to say that you can't change superficial things. You need to find your positive attributes and "polish" them so you'll be more likely to attract Mr. Right instead of Mr. Right now. A good place to start is with your health, hygiene, and attitude. You can also brush up on your conversation skills and educate yourself. I'm not saying you have to enroll at Harvard, but you can read and make your knowledge base more well-rounded. Not many men want a relationship with someone who can't carry on an intelligent conversation.

Many women focus solely on the man's qualifications when they're trying to find their life mate. The reality is that you must also have good qualities as well. A relationship is a two-way street in every sense. Do you qualify?

I'm sorry to inform you ladies but whatever your preference is, you must qualify as well —there's a of competition out. Yes, believe it or not, you're competing whether you realize it or not.

For those who believe there isn't a competition taking place, I strongly advise you to prepare for the leftovers. A perfect example of the competition is when a woman prepares herself for an evening out at a club or heavily populated venue. She's not really preparing for the men she'll see, she's making sure she can "beat" the other women in attendance. I'm not saying that the women don't notice the men, but their focus is on the possible competition in the room.

Subconsciously, women know it's a competition and they're all serious competitors! Take my advice, ladies, and give yourself that extra edge so you can find Mr. Right and keep him!

Get the One You Want!!
(No one cares but you!)

Have you ever seen a sweet little lady walking a nasty pit bull or other ferocious dog? Did you wonder, "How did she end up with that dog?"

Have you ever seen a large man with a little bitty housedog and wondered the exact same thing?

After seeing either of these scenarios a few times, all you can do is laugh at the oddity of it all. You don't have time to really care how they ended up together or try to figure it out because you don't have to deal with it. You subconsciously decide that this pairing must fit their needs and you move on.

The same rules should be applied to women's choice of men. If you like a Pit Pull, go for it! Ultimately you're the only one who has to deal with him on a daily basis.

News flash: People will make comments about your choice, but no one really has time to care too much. They don't really have time to worry about another person's relationship oddities.

I promise you; late at night when you close the door to your residence you won't be able to hear their comments. So, if this is the fit that's right for your situation and don't worry about getting public approval for your decision.

Who knows? You may want a short, boring, talkative, hairy man in your life. Whatever floats your boat! Public opinion should never matter because the people who are voicing all the opinions usually don't have to live your life and probably don't have much going on in theirs. That's why they're so interested in telling you what to do with yours.

The next time you see the lady with the big pit bull say to yourself, "Go ahead, girl!" As long as you're not the one cleaning up the poop, what does it matter to you? It doesn't!

When selecting a dog, you know what you want, why you may want him, and you just get him. Use the same logic with a man. You need to make sure you get what you want because it's your prerogative. Ultimately you need to get what makes you happy!

Some people have ugly dogs but they are the most proud owners. Why? Because they got exactly what they wanted!

Evolution of Man

If a man stars out life as a German Shepherd, it doesn't necessarily mean he will stay that breed. Men can evolve and move breeds due to life experiences that cause them alter their lifestyles and possibly their personality traits. This evolution can occur because of a bad relationship experience or he can be influenced by other things he's seen, heard and done over the years.

An example of the cause of this type of evolution is dealing with a relationship where a German Shepherd's woman cheated on him. The relationship ended because of this infidelity, and he evolves because of what he's gone through. He definitely won't be as trusting in his next relationship and might even unintentionally take out his anger at his previous woman on his new lady.

Because of his experience, he's had a hard dose of reality and now realizes that everyone isn't as honest and caring as he is. He might start to see duplicity in his next relationship, in friendships, and even in his daily encounters. His world has been rocked, and not in a good way!

This negative experience will make him exhibit new, less German Shepherd-like traits. Whether he is worse than before or better will be decided by how well he ultimately deals with this betrayal and subsequent evolution. Some men subconsciously like a little pain and suffering and will be able to get on with their lives relatively easily. Others don't want to experience these feelings even a little bit and will be forever changed by living through them on such a personal level. Either way, they will know the signs of deceit when they see them again, and will have to decide to confront or ignore them.

That example is an extreme case, but evolution can also come about through slow erosion. For example, if a dog's woman behaves negatively or nags him all the time, this will wear on him until he eventually evolves because of it.

To a certain degree, the woman controls the joystick that decides her man's evolution — and that change doesn't always have to be negative. Your dog categorizes each of his experiences as a warning, a treat, or an all-out reward. Things like positive reinforcement can make for a positive evolution, i.e. all-out reward for you both.

Now that you know how this works, ladies, you can take some time to re-evaluate the way you approach situations with your dog. Be sure that everything you do leans toward the positive, because he might take the negative a run with it in a direction you do not want him to go.

Beware, the evolution process is not an easy one for your dog. You don't want to lose him through a communication breakdown during this process, so be patient with him and take a deep breath before laying down anything negative. You're building a better man here, so you need to be careful how you proceed.

One benefit to the evolution process can be that he starts to like the treats and positive reinforcement and will work hard to do things to earn that from you. This may also make him way less willing to stray. When another potential dog owner offers him a treat, he may look at it, smell it, or kick it for a reaction but in the end he's not going to go for it because he loves the treats you give him at home.

Now this isn't the case in every instance, because some dogs just can't help themselves. That doesn't mean he doesn't like your treats, it's just how he is.

Again I'll say it — it is what it is. You must understand what breed you're dealing with so you'll know what you can expect.

Puppies/the Puppy Trap

P uppies (babies) are adorable, cute, cuddly, and loving. They also require a lot of immediate attention, care, and affection. The minute you decide to enter into a physical relationship with someone, you must be aware of the possible consequences — having a puppy (baby) means a lot of responsibilities and the potential to create a new life is always there when you're intimate. So, don't take that decision lightly.

Some women try to use puppies as a way to trap men into long-term commitments — a method I call the puppy trap. The woman uses the child to try to force the man into becoming her long-term mate. Some women even go so far as to plan the specific genetic traits they want their babies to have, including hair color and type, even complexion. I've actually heard women say they wanted their baby to look a certain way and picked a mate so they could achieve that look. Isn't that a feeble-minded way to select a father for your child?

The puppy trap can be set and sprung in a variety of ways. We will only discuss two methods here. The first method is just being negligent and/or unprotected during the relationship. The woman subliminally hopes for a slip-up that will trap the man and force him to stay around for the long haul.

Other women think having a puppy will help calm their man's actions, slow him down and scare him straight. In some rare cases may work this way, but nine times out of ten it does nothing more than delay the inevitable! Like the old saying goes, "You can't keep anybody that don't want to be kept!"

Having the puppy may initially seem to make your bond stronger and make your dog abruptly man up to his responsibilities as a father. As the child grows up, though, your dog will start to feel the feelings he felt before this world changer started.

Ladies, you need to realize that just because he loves his child more than life itself does not mean he feels the same way about you. Nor does it mean he will step up his game and become a responsible person. So, be careful with your motives and attempts to use the puppy trap to get what you want. It may turn into an epic fail!

The second method for the puppy trap is the heinous, despicable method of deliberately getting pregnant to trap your dog into financial obligations. Worse still, is attempting to obtain your financial freedom by purposely and maliciously setting your dog up. This is a desperation move by a woman who wants to gain some of that particular dog's success and/or fortune.

These women will try anything from turkey basters to puncturing condoms, saving specimens, and other little evil tricks to get to a comfortable position in life. It saddens me to admit that this method has worked, especially on athletes. Many dogs have no clue about what their lady has planned for them.

I speak for all dogs when I say this type of thing can happen to the best of us. No one is totally immune. However, just because it happens doesn't mean the woman gets exactly what she was trying for. Her plan a cushy, long-term relationship probably has a shelf life — and she has to work for it every day so her trapped man doesn't decide it's not worth it and bolt. The burden of maintaining this little fiction will fall completely on the game runner.

I say good luck to those who run this game because in the future, Karma's gonna get you! Your payback is gift-wrapped with a big bow on it waiting for you on down the line. It could be that you suddenly find you're the one who's trapped because you have to live with a pure A-hole because your dog realizes what you did and he's lashing out. After it's all said and done, you'll have to ask yourself if it was really worth it.

'Euthanizing' Him Might Come Back to Bite You

Statistics show that nine out of ten people have experienced a breakup. Emotional damage is inevitable in most breakups. When pain, humiliation, disloyalty, or mental/physical abuse occurs because of that breakup, many women jump on the retaliation bandwagon.

That retaliation might take the form of what I call the Euthanization method. This method is when a woman does everything in her power to annihilate and pretty much castrate the man who wronged her. This means anything from having sex with one of his closest friends to calling his family and telling them personal details. This method is not new, but lately it seems to be contagious and spreading at a rapid rate.

Recently, it's even been praised and given the seal of approval by the general public. You see it in movies, hear it in songs, and read about it in books and poems. A quick example of this is the song "Bust Your Windows!" by Jasmine Sullivan. You may be saying to yourself, "Well, he deserved what he got and maybe a little more."

These vengeful women use the Euthanizing method to attack a man's spirit, pride, and possibly his wallet, too. I admit that some men deserve an ass whipping for the pain, anguish, and wasted years they inflicted on their former mates, but two wrongs don't make a right!

These women aren't satisfied until they see their version of Karma in action. What women must understand is true Karma works on its own schedule. When you take matters into your own hands, what you're doing has nothing to do with Karma — you're getting revenge, and that can put the Karmic ball right back in your court.

The most damaging version of the Euthanizing method is using the kids against him by keeping them from him, continuously talking trash about him in the kids' presence, and ultimately trying to turn them against him. Doing this means you've gone too far! The kids should never be the pawns in this nasty game. The children should be allowed to make their own decisions without undue influence from you.

If play the "your daddy's no good" game, it could also backfire and end up making you the bad guy in your kids' eyes. Pointing out all of daddy's flaws can help to point out your own. This ploy really doesn't work in your favor and it only confuses and alienates the children. Plus, if you keep this up long-term, in the future the children might end up resenting you for a relationship that has been over for years. Here comes Karma again!

You should remember what Matthew 7 says, "Do not judge so that you will not be judged. For in the way you judge, you will be judged and by your standard of measure it will be measured to you. Why do you look at the speck that is in your brother's eye, but do not noticed the log that is in your own eye?"

Regardless of your religious beliefs, this applies to everyone.

If you can't get around using the Euthanizing method, then be prepared — it will hurt you just as much as you hurt him.

THE HEALING PROCESS

Whether it's a little stunt or a big one, when you've finished with your Euthanization project you're going to have to go through a healing process. This process will take you on a roller coaster ride of emotions including anger, denial, sadness, fear (of starting over), etc. You may also find yourself living in a dark place. If you're not careful at this point, you can lose yourself and turn all that anger and pain inward.

Examples of this self-abuse could include sleeping with a guy who wouldn't have had a snowball's chance in Texas heat of getting with you if you weren't on this self-destructive path. You might also start binging, using food or alcohol to try to fill that emptiness you feel to your soul. This is a dangerous path!

Friends might try to cheer you up and offer their two cents worth of usually worthless advice about your situation, but their cheerleading goes home when they do and you're alone yet again.

If you find yourself feeling isolated, use that isolation to bring about a revelation. This is your time to reveal yourself to yourself. Use this time to think and prepare for living your life. Focus on your goals and keep an open mind during the process. You never know where life will take you once you've settled into your own skin!

Taking this route of self-discovery will help you to stop feeling like you totally lost yourself and the structure that gives you your identity and self-respect when you lost the relationship. You'll come to realize that damaging your ex's material possessions or his reputation can hurt him for a while, but he'll eventually get on with his life. If you can't do the same, then you're making him stronger and ultimately rendering yourself powerless. Use this experience to build yourself up rather than tearing him down! In the end, it's you who will have to make the decision to get yourself together and move on.

SEEING YOUR EX AGAIN

There is nothing worse than seeing your ex looking good, changed for the better, with a different attitude and mind set, being the guy you'd always wished he would be. Even if you don't want him, you say to yourself, "Why wasn't he like that when we were together?"

Maybe he couldn't change while you were together because you weren't giving him what he needed to make those changes. Yeah, it's deep! If he'd been an actual canine that wrecked your house, pooped on the floor, and chewed up your favorite shoes, you wouldn't have euthanized him for this bad behavior, but you would probably take him to the local SPCA and let him go. You need to do the same for the man. The key is don't ever look back.

The worst thing you could do is let him back into your life. You might think that never seeing him again will hurt more than letting him back in. The thing is, those times he's around will be at his convenience — this includes bending for those lonely nights and a little maintenance. Doing this allows your dog to roam free and only return to you when he feels like it. In other words, you're letting him have his cake and eat it too!

I call this the little by little method. This method will eventually breed the hurt that turns to hatred and leads to the Euthanizing method. You've put yourself in a place where you're going to get hurt repeatedly. Each of those injuries will pile up until all you want to do is hurt him in return.

It's so much better to just walk away and let another owner deal with his mess. You're probably wondering, *Why should I?* You should let another owner deal with his mess because you're wasting your time with him and could be missing your chance at meeting Mr. Right in the process. You're letting his baggage and lingering presence keep you from your future!

You also need to realize that pounding his brains in with a bat to let him know how much grief and pain he's caused you isn't really accomplishing anything. The best way to make him realize the damage he's done is to walk away without another word. Wondering why you didn't try to get him back will be a nice little bit of mental torture for him. It will eat away at his confidence, deflate his ego and make him question his powers of attraction. This can have a greater effect on him than anything you do to him physically.

Men are logical thinkers so he'll try his best to wrap his mind around what just happened. It will be hard for him to believe that you could just walk away from him without putting up a fight. Trust me, it will be a serious lesson learned for him. The key is to do it quickly and completely, like ripping off a Band-Aid.

FINDING A NEW DOG AND LETTING GO

This book is designed to help you understand that there are numerous factors that can turn what you may think should be a sure thing into a nightmare. It could be influences like drugs, alcohol, addictions, his upbringing and morals, family values, lack of discipline, and most importantly a differing belief system. Men are fixed creatures just like dogs, and they're not as difficult to under-stand as you might think.

Each man's character traits work to make him an individual. You're not going to have much changing those — that's up to him. *All Men Are Dogs* was also designed to help you understand how you can refine your selection process and increase your odds of finding the right dog for you. When you find a dog you think might be right for you, be sure you think about the following:

- What he may or may not bring to the table

- What he needs from you

- Your qualifications for being his owner

- How to coexist with him

- How to remain calm if things don't work out

Using this third eye information is designed to help you change your mindset. It will also to help you to "weed out" the dogs who just won't be a good fit for you as well as helping you to recognize the good ones. This way you won't waste time trying to train the wrong dog or find yourself running from a good thing. You'll have the skills to find what's right for you.

So, forget that old dog, make your plan and get out there so you can find the dog of your dreams!

24

Dogs to Men

This book was a good way to trick you into thinking of men in a negative way. Many in the world try to condition women to think a certain about men. Yes, men *are* like dogs. They are similar in characteristics and traits.

Since the world we live in is based on a profit system it can be frustrating for a man to achieve his goal of providing a comfortable life for his mate and family. He must be able to juggle all of this as well as try to keep himself in shape and competitive on all fronts. This need to compete can stress a man to the breaking point.

Most men feel this need to "Keep up with the Joneses" and worry that they will become outcasts or seem unworthy if they don't. They're also afraid you will lose interest if they "fall behind" in this imagined race.

This does not take anything away from the daily struggles women face. We're just trying to see things through the eyes of the dog-man. While society as a whole tries to perpetuate a different story, men usually still feel this age-old need to "provide" for their woman.

This can be mentally, physically and emotionally draining for a man. Many times he's trying to keep up financially and even physically with someone of celebrity status and just ends up exhausting himself because he's reaching for these unrealistic goals. Doing this just puts him at a great disadvantage.

What he doesn't realize is that many of the iconic celebrities he's idolizing wouldn't have much if you took away the money and material items it buys. The reality is that probably only a handful would have their mate at their side if he were just an ordinary guy. This is sad but it is true.

So, ladies, here's the scoop: men have doubts, insecurities, and unrealistic goals. They might act like they've got it all together, but chances are, they don't!

You might meet a man who seems to be a good match for you, but he's shy around women, has trouble socializing, etc. Do you give up on him and move on or do you help him move from a dog to a man?

Could it be that it takes a good woman to make a good man? Rather than denigrate men in general, maybe it would be better to try to understand them and help them become what they aspire to.

One of the core differences that distinguishes a real man from all the dogs is his ability to control himself and make choices that may be contrary to his feelings of the moment. It's all about self-control and self-discipline. Help you dog learn that he can make choices and sacrifices to gain something of greater worth.

When your dog learns that attaining his goals may take many hours of practice, sacrificing less important activities, etc. he will learn the value of self-discipline. The same thing goes for accountability. Holding him accountable for his responsibilities to teach him how to be responsible. This is not an easy process for you or him, but it will be well worth the time.

Sometimes as men rebel a bit at all of the rules and consequences in their lives and long for the days when they had more freedom. If they give in to these feelings, then they'll surely misbehave. Living in a world of rules and consequences is a reality you need to help your dog embrace. So help your dog commit to living by the rules at home and impose consequences when he makes bad choices. If you don't establish those rules in the beginning, you and dog could face problems later.

Try to teach your dog compassion. The perception that a man has to be emotionless and conceal his feelings is real, but harmful to quality relationships. Teach him the importance of kindness and compassion, showing love. These feelings will balance his life and take him from a dog to a responsible, loving man.

You're probably asking, *Are there any* perfect *men out there?* Probably not. You need to "build" your own and teaching by example so that he will become the man of your dreams.

Do not get forgiveness twisted with forgetfulness or being naïve.

Forgive but *Do Not* Forget the Dog!!!

Forgiving another can be the most challenging and gut-wrenching task you may have to ever face, especially if you've been hurt badly. However, once forgiveness is truly achieved it can also be healing, humbling, rewarding, and insightful for a man.

Forgiveness is humbling because it allows you to take a step back and observe the situation without the emotional knee-jerk reaction that can cause you to retaliate or seek retribution for the hurt they inflicted upon you. While the thought of retribution might seem like the cure for your hurt, it's only a short-term fix and it can cause long-term damage. You need something long-term that will let you move on with your life.

Forgiveness can be rewarding because this release can be beneficial and healing to your mind, body, and soul. It helps to transfer negative energy from your body. This release can help to clear your cloudy judgment, and help you to make better decisions so you can get your life back. Releasing all of this negativity also lets you leave all the baggage behind so you'll be open to a new relationship in the future.

In a sense, without true forgiveness you can be blocking your own blessing. You must realize that this negative energy can prevent you from achieving your true purpose in life. If you hold on to these bad feelings, ultimately they affect all aspects of your life, from relationships to your job status, and most importantly your body's state of homeostasis or balance.

However, do not get forgiveness twisted with forgetfulness or being naïve. Once you've forgiven, don't forget what happened and fall into the same trap again, and certainly don't let intimacy back you into an all too familiar corner. It's easy to go back to what you know, but it's a dead end. He's already proved that to you, and you don't need a repeat performance! Never forget what a dog your man has been.

This is why forgiving the dog should happen, but be handled carefully. What you've experienced because of this dog shouldn't make you a bitter man-hater — a bitter root produces a bitter fruit. Learn from this experience so that you don't end up in this place again. This attitude will help you enter your next situation with open eyes and a renewed sense of yourself. Turn this negatives experience into a positive life-lesson and view it as a blessing in disguise. This isn't easy work, but will be more than worth it to you.

Once you've come to this realization, you'll be able to smile and know that you have been blessed with the gift of the third eye. The third eye helps you to see things what you might not have seen before and helps you to make better choices in your life.

If you are in a relationship where you were required to forgive someone and decided to give it another chance, it makes no sense to always be on guard, bracing for a second blow that may come. If you cannot truly get back to your life and stop obsessing about what might happen, you'll be living an unhappy life that could ultimately affect your health and age you in the process. Be confident in your decision and allow your third eye to keep watch for you as you get on with living your life. Remember, love can be a two-edged sword — it can be great or it can make you hate. Don't be a hater.

The definition of insanity is doing the same thing over and over and expecting different results. Learn from your experiences so that you don't make certain mistakes again. Forgive him, forgive yourself and move on to something positive. Some things in life are worth fighting for, i.e. you! Pick yourself up, dust off the rust, and go at it again with the knowledge from the past to make it right on the next go 'round.

In the situation where there is physical violence, the next step needs to be an exit!

26

Beware of the Dog

Unfortunately violence is a part of some relationships. Most women don't know how to recognize a potentially abusive situation, and many are surprised when things progress to the point of violence.

So, ladies, please beware of the dog. Domestic violence is often swept under the rug and people are reluctant to discuss it. I'm going to discuss it here so that you won't find yourself caught off guard and will be able to spot the telltale signs leading to this behavior.

First, one must understand that there is usually a prelude to violent behavior. Notice I said usually. It may take a long time before it progresses to the point of actual violence; however, the signs are always there. No matter which dog breed you call your own, the potential for violent behavior can be there. So, never take it for granted that your dog won't turn on you this way.

What can get you into trouble is delaying action once you see the signs. The indecisiveness comes into play because you just can't believe it's true. This usually leaves you in a state of confusion and false hope that "it won't happen again." The potential for violence was there all along; the dog was just good at hiding it ... until he wasn't. Don't fool yourself — if it happened once, chances are it will happen again.

If you are in a relationship where your man lays his hands on you, then this should be all you need to know it's time to make a run for the hills. Normally I'm the last person to recommend leaving a relationship because my belief is that everyone has the free will to define his or her own happiness, but in this instance, the *only* next step is to make your exit!

If you don't believe me, let me break it down in dog terms. Let's say you get a dog and bring him home. At some point down the line, he attacks you. Do you keep him around so he can possibly do it again?

There were probably warning signs with the attacking dog, just as there were warning signs with the abusive man. If your man has a temperament that is irritable, impulsive and aggressive then you should be careful, especially if his aggressive behavior causes intentional physical or emotional harm to others, or threatens to. This behavior can range from verbal to physical abuse.

Abuse can take many forms, including:

- **Physical abuse** like hitting, shoving, kicking, biting, or throwing things
- **Emotional abuse** like yelling, controlling what you do, or threatening to cause serious problems for you
- **Sexual abuse** like forcing you to do something sexual you don't want to do

Take a long, honest look at your relationship. Are you focusing all your energy on your partner, dropping friends and family or activities you enjoy, feeling pressured or controlled, having more bad times in the relationship than good, and feeling sad or scared when with your partner? Do you really want to live this way? Will it only get worse?

When you realize your relationship is an abusive one, it does not mean you should have it out with him. Don't get in the dog's face and make threats with your brothers and guy friends to back you up. This type of behavior will just provoke him and make things worse. The best way to handle the situation is calmly and rationally. Make a plan for yourself and carry it out. There is never any excuse for a man to put his hands on a female and vice versa. No one deserves to be abused.

If your dog won't let you handle things calmly or if his behavior escalates, you might need to get some outside help.*

---

*If the relationship has progressed to the point that you are afraid for your safety, you should contact the National Domestic Violence Hotline (800-799-7233) for assistance in locating programs in your area.

The Bible describes a dual obligation in which mutual obligations and respect for each other are required. (Ephesians 5:21-32)

'27'

'Submit' to the Dog

Women usually cringe at the use of the word submit. I would like to address the subject of submissiveness. Since this book is about adjusting your perspective, words should be looked at in context.

The meaning I'm going for here is the duel obligation of the relationship. It's the actual boundaries that are set between both parties. Submissiveness should not be looked upon as a sign of weakness; instead it should be looked upon as being humble. By humble, I mean that your needs should not always come first in the relationship; you should also respect the needs of your mate.

Being humble in this way is the active ingredient in any relationship. Remembering this can smooth out miscommunications, prevent words that can't be taken back, and stop small misunderstanding from destroying the trust and bond you have established.

This is explained in your _Basic Instructions Before Leaving Earth_ manual, aka the Bible. It describes a dual obligation in which mutual respect for each other is required. (Ephesians 5:21-32) Whether you are a religious person or not, being humble in this way and having mutual respect in your relationship is a good thing!

This respect comes from working at the relationship and involves the same message I've been preaching all along — communication. Without communication you have nothing. You can't respect someone when you have no clue what they're about. We all have differences and you owe it to your relationship find out what they are so you can understand each other.

Couples make the mistake of assuming they know their mates and never take the time to actually talk to them and learn the truth. Without this effective communication, before long you're literally in a relationship with a complete stranger. When I say effective, I mean you must find a method that works for your relationship. Some couples write things out and others can just talk.

Here are a few tips to get you started:

- **Find the right time.** If something is bothering you and you want to have a serious conversation about it, make sure you pick the right time to talk. Don't interrupt your partner when they're watching sports game or a favorite TV show, etc.

- **Talk face to face**. Avoid talking about serious matters or issues in text messages or emails — they can be misinterpreted. Talk in person so there is no confusion or misinterpretation.

- **Do not attack.** Watch your word choice. Using "you" sounds like you're attacking, which will make your partner defensive and less receptive. Instead, try using "I" or "we." For example, say "I feel we haven't been as close lately" instead of "You've been distant."

- **Be honest.** Sometimes the truth hurts, but it's the key to a healthy relationship. You should also be able to admit when you're wrong.

- **Undivided attention.** Make eye contact when speaking and let him know you're listening and you care. Don't take a phone call, text or play a video game when you're talking. (He should do the same.)

- **Let it sit.** If your partner does something that makes you angry, tell him about it but not necessarily right away. If you're still hurt 48 hours later, say something. If not, forget about it.

- **Not a mind reader.** Remember, your partner can't read your mind. If you don't speak up when you're upset, there is no way for him to apologize or change.

- **Let it go.** Once you do mention your hurt feelings and your partner sincerely apologies, let it go. Don't bring up past issues.

- **If you're really angry.** Stop, take a step back and breathe and give yourself time to calm down. Think about why you got so angry. Figure out the real problem and explain your feelings. When you talk to your partner, follow the tips above.

- **Listen.** After you tell your partner how you feel, remember to stop talking and listen to what they have to say. Remember, you both deserve the opportunity to express your feelings.

Both men and women need to understand what they are dealing with while in a relationship, and to do this they have to communicate. This communication needs to be a *constant* concern; because our brains are always learning and developing new ideas that help us evolve a little each day. You will also need to *consistently* discuss these new ideas and changes in yourself with your partner. Note how they have caused you to change, both emotionally and intellectually. Keeping these lines of communication open will lead to a better understanding of each other's want and needs and will ultimately be worth your efforts.

Just remember, the key to relationship happiness is constant, consistent, communication.

The Dog Rules!

I f you've turned up your nose at the title of this section and thought, *No Dog rules me!* then your perception of things may be your reality. Just as you need to know how to care for a dog before you owning it, there are things women need to learn during their pre-dog (pre-relationship) life.

These Dog Rules are key to keeping things together for the duration of the relationship. Even if you're involved in a relationship now, the Dog Rules can help to refresh and reinforce your bond.

If you're truly in search of love, you must understand the meaning of the term. The definition of love is: a strong affection for another arising out of kinship or personal ties; affection based on admiration. The Bible describes the word love in 1 Corinthians 13:4-8: "Love is patient and kind; love does not envy or boast, it is not proud. It does not dishonor others, it is not self-seeking, it is not easily angered, it keeps no record of wrongs. Love does not delight in evil but rejoices with the truth. It always protects, always trusts, always hopes, always perseveres. Love never fails."

These two definitions from two different sources agree that love is responsibility between two people. Your patience, kindness, temperament, humbleness, truth, loyalty, trust, and will to persevere will be tested on all levels in a relationship, no matter what dog you choose. Your ability to respond to each situation as it presents itself, is the deal maker or deal breaker.

In this book, I've used the various dog breeds as a clever way to shed light on the serious topic of relationships. Whether its girlfriend/boyfriend or husband/wife our relationships can make us or break us — literally.

Only you and your partner can make the decisions that will balance your life together and lead you to happiness. Conversely, you are also the only ones who can upset that balance.

If you look at the news — 850,000 divorces filed, nearly 1.3 million women and about 835,000 men assaulted by their partners, more than 1000 murder/suicides, and countless bad breakups — you'll see that we aren't doing a good job of balancing our lives. We, as a country, have a serious problem and it is growing at an epidemic rate. It's time we all get busy and resolve our issues starting with our romantic relationships.

The solution to this dog-gone problem is first-hand information. You obtain this information from the dog himself, from using your eyes and ears to observe his actions. You cannot just try to "think like a man" and figure it out. There are two of you in the relationship — man and woman — and you think differently.

This is where the Dog Rules come into play. They are as follows:

- **Respect the Dog.** This is the first rule, because respect is at the core of a dog's pride. Respect is the scale balancer in a relationship. Respect and communication go hand in hand to help determine your dog's boundaries. Never assume anything because you never know how your dog might react to something that you feel is insignificant.

- **Appreciate the dog.** All dogs love appreciation. Appreciate his worth — you can do this by not making your dog feel small. Appreciate his need to provide, even if you make more income than him. Appreciate what he brings to the table.

- **Recognize the dog's leadership and insight.** Whether he has innate leadership qualities or not, make him feel like he does. Not all dogs will lead in the right direction but the great thing about being his mate is that you can help to steer him on the correct course. You can also cultivate his leadership qualities and help to make him into a leader.

- **Breathe life into the dog.** It would be wise to encourage and believe in him. This encouragement can help cultivate not only him but also build your respect for one another.

- **Keep your identity.** Never try to recreate yourself. I'm not saying change is necessarily bad, but you should tell your dog about your newfound goals so you'll be on the same page.

- **Be your dog's best friend.** The best thing you can do is be a friend to your dog. In the complex world we live in sometimes a dog needs a place of peace. Being a friend to your dog allows him to express himself naturally. This will also help you to understand the dog's highs, lows, and where he is mentally, sometimes without him even barking a word. Friendship fortifies the foundation of a good relationship!

The Dog Rules are not difficult to accomplish, but they do require work. The level of challenge and trials you will encounter depend on the dog you choose. Having the knowledge provided here can help you to find a mate or rejuvenate a fading situation and can ultimately aid you in your quest for happiness.

You must realize it's a dog-eat-dog world out there and you might not find your right dog the first time around. There's a lot of pressures on dogs to act like something they're not, so the dog you thought you had can end up being someone else entirely and you have to move. Other times, you'll just have to let a sleeping dog lie, because some dogs aren't worth the trouble — you lay down some dogs, you might wake up with fleas!

Once you've found your dog, if he happens to make a mistake there is nothing wrong with him being in the doghouse for a minute. This will give you both the time you need to think about things. Be calm and decide if you should move on without him or move forward with him.

While it's true you can't teach an old dog new tricks, with the proper communication and mutual respect you can modify your dog's behavior. This is what will build the good relationship that all your friends wish they had when they witness the respect and adoration you and your dog display.

You've learned that love is not about 'fixing' your dog. You embraced his unique qualities, and found the real deal — love!

It would be nice if all dogs had a six pack, an extremely large bank account, were great listeners, had a great career, were non-cheaters and were also willing to go with you to try on shoes. ☺ Ha! That's only happens on television.

The real fun in life is finding that special dog and living for the good times. It's riding out the bad times and taking advantage of creating memories. Now, go out there and find your perfect dog!

Acknowledgements

GOD is my Father who guides me throughout my life.

- David and Genevieve Elliott (parents)
- Kaysha and Dominique Elliott (kids)
- Ashley Rampersaud
- Roland Veal Jr.& Tisha Veal
- Rayne and Landon Veal
- David Elliott III
- David IV & Imani Elliott (nephew/niece)
- Jessica Goodbee (Graphic Designer)
- Marchet Denise Fullum (Editor)
- Benjamin and Linda Allen
- Benjamin Allen Jr.
- Demetrius Allen
- Elodie Allen (RIP)
- Richard Allen (RIP)
- Maude Elliott (RIP)
- David Elliott (RIP)
- Richard and Carolyn Allen
- Chris, Brandon, Jonathon Allen
- Lisette and Lartigue Porche
- Lil Teague Porche
- Joseph and Antoinette Lewis
- Brittney and JC Lewis
- Theresa Sabathia
- Michelle and Chop Epps
- Ashley Sabathia
- Lisa and Ernest Hakim
- Delither Allen
- Bird and Debra Yarbrough
- Javon and Darlene Yarbrough
- Lil J. (Javon), Delana Yarbrough
- Sherrell Yarbrough
- Dr. Sabrina Echols
- Kavon Moore
- Alisa Shelton
- Millette Womack Spiller
- Patricia Womack
- Phillip and Betty Luke
- Lejeaune and Lair Womack
- Donald and Brandy McGraw
- Mable Julian
- Warren (Butch) Thomas
- Kirk Thomas
- Dr. Eugene Nunnery
- Yvette & Amya Nunnery
- Joyce Bell (RIP)
- Dr. Debra Katz
- Mark and Dena Parrott
- Rick and Gwen Stinson
- Myracle Primus
- Joe Black Barbershop (Houston)
- David and Debbie Preisler
- Robin Surface
- & whoever else I forgot to mention. I love you all!

www.ingramcontent.com/pod-product-compliance
Lightning Source LLC
Chambersburg PA
CBHW032119040426
42449CB00005B/198